Project Management Handbook

Project Management Handbook

Houman John Parsaie, Ph.D.

Writers Club Press
San Jose New York Lincoln Shanghai

Project Management Handbook

Writers Club Press
an imprint of iUniverse, Inc.

For information address:
iUniverse, Inc.
5220 S. 16th St., Suite 200
Lincoln, NE 68512
www.iuniverse.com

ISBN: 0-595-22073-8

Printed in the United States of America

CONTENTS

PREFACE

This manual has been written to help those preparing for the PMP Examination. It is intended to cover all of the material that the Project Management Institute (PMI) considers important enough to be included in the PMP exam. However, this manual may also be used as reference material for certified PMP's and/or other project managers in virtually any field or industry.

If project management is practiced using the methodology outlined in this manual and the PMI's *Guide to the Project Management Body of Knowledge*, you will become a great project manager. Learning project management is more than studying a book or even a group of books and literatures. Project management must also be learned in the field with experience and exposure to real responsibility on real projects. The Project Management Professional (PMP) certification is designed to certify project managers who meet both the criteria for knowledge and experience. To qualify for certification, you must have both. PMI requires that you have at least 4,500 hours of experience if you have earned a bachelor's degree. Some of this experience must extend past more than the last three years but no more than six years. If you do not have earned a bachelor's degree, you must have at least 7,500 hours within the last eight years. Starting year 2002, PMI is introducing a new certification program, where you still can be certified as an associate project manager, if you do not have enough experience (i.e. you have less than 4,500 hours with a bachelor's degree or 7,500 hours without one, respectively).

This book is intended to cover all the subject matters of the PMP exam. Since the PMP exam is a comprehensive examination of your knowledge of project management tools and techniques, it is not possible to find all the answers to all the questions on the PMP exam in this book; nor is it in any other book or a single source. PMI is constantly changing the examination. They are constantly introducing new questions and replacing questions that have been around for some time.

It is my opinion that no one should be able to pass the PMP examination without extremely good and thorough working knowledge of the practice of project management. I have tried in this book to explain the nature of project management, how all of the techniques and tools relate to one another, and how they all go together to make up a unified methodology that can be used to successfully managing projects.

Houman John Parsaie, Ph.D.
December 2001, Seattle, Washington

INTRODUCTION

What is Project Management?
PMP Certification

What is Project Management?

The *Guide to the PMBOK* defines project management as follows: "Project Management is the application of knowledge, skills, and techniques to project activities in order to meet or exceed stakeholder needs and expectations from a project." Thus, project management is utilizing a set of tools and techniques to manage projects more effectively. In order to understand this better, we should define what a project is:

The *Guide to the PMBOK* defines project as follows: "Project is a temporary endeavor undertaken to provide a unique product or service." *Temporary* means that any project completed must have a beginning and an end. A project must have some sort of definite beginning and some sort of definite end. Generally, a project begins when an official document proclaims the project to have an official life. This document usually creates some means of budget for the project. The end of the project is usually when all of the project goals have been met and all of the work of the project has been accomplished. Some projects end when for various reasons it has been decided to abandon the project and stop work on it. This is generally because the goals of the project cannot be practically achieved.

Some distinction is made between the words *project* and *program*. Most project managers feel that the project management profession can manage projects of any size and that the methodology that is used to manage them all is nearly the same, with modifications made to accommodate different sized projects. The methods and steps used in the project management process are the same.

According to the *Guide to the PMBOK*, a program is a group of projects managed in a coordinated way to obtain benefits that may not be obtained, if managed separately. This definition is familiar when we speak of very large programs, but all projects are really subprojects of larger projects or are composed of subprojects. From the perspective of a subproject manager, he or she is in charge of these several subprojects, he or she is responsible for his or her own project. The difficulty of this definition is that there is no clear distinction between the size of a project and a program. It is also true that in some organizations, programs may even be considered to be subprojects of other projects. All of this goes to show that project management is not a strict science but has some artistic aspects to it as well. We will see that there are many differences in terminology throughout the project management profession. PMI has made a remarkable effort to try to separate and standardize this terminology.

It is important to realize that the end of the project is not the same as the end of the goods and services that the project produces. A project to build a power plant usually ends when the goal of building the plant and making it operable to produce some expected level of production has been achieved. The plant continues to operate far into the future even though the project has ended.

Projects are always unique in many ways. This is not to say that projects are totally and completely unique, since many projects build on the results of other projects and have many things in common with other projects that the organization has completed in the past. A project is unique because there is something that sets this project apart from others. If it were not for this uniqueness, the project would not be a project—it would be a routine repetition of something done before and would not require many of the project management tools and techniques.

Projects are "progressively elaborated," which means that the products of a project are progressively developed throughout the project. The goals and objectives of a project are started at the beginning of the project. These goals and objectives are elaborated and made clearer by the project team and become more detailed as the project progresses.

Projects generally have certain types of characteristics that make them unique. Projects are going to be always temporary-endeavors, because they are intentionally put together with the purpose of accomplishing specific tasks. Once these specific tasks have been accomplished, the resources that were put together for this purpose can be assigned to other projects. This means that the people and resources from other project(s) can be brought together and formed for another project.

In modern project management, project teams bring together resources as they are required. One of the great advantages to project management is its ability to form multidisciplined project teams of the right people at the right time. The obvious advantage of this is that scarce skills can be brought to a project when needed.

Projects always have limited resources, but sometimes there are projects where the cost and amount of resources seem to be unlimited. To the project manager who is trying to get a project completed with scarce or unavailable resources, it might seem wonderful to manage a project with unlimited resources. But these types of projects usually come with severe schedule requirements.

Projects are finished when their goal has been accomplished. It follows that the goal is accomplished for a person or organization that has something at stake in the results of the project. These persons are called "stakeholders." Projects often have more than one stakeholder, and each of the stakeholders has different needs and expectations.

The "client" or "customer" or "sponsor" is a special kind of stakeholder in projects. This is the main stakeholder. Without this stakeholder the project probably would not go forward. This is usually the one that puts up the money for the project and has the most interest in its success. Thus, we can now say that project management is the application of the tools and techniques that are necessary to satisfy the expectations of the stakeholder(s) of the project.

"Of course, I don't look busy—I did it right the first time." This one sentence brings to mind the problem that so many of us face in implementing project-management strategies and methods in our businesses. It seems that people are resistant to change even when it is good for them, and they do not appreciate people who get things done if they don't look busy enough. As a newly certified project management professional, you will undoubtedly run into some resistance when you try to implement new ideas, and project management techniques are full of new ideas. You must be polite and persistence, if you have confidence in yourself and ideas you have.

There is a story that I really believe it is true about a project manager who went to work for a company that produced computer software. It turns out that this project manager was hired to complete a project that was to produce a significant amount of the company's income for the year, and it had a strict deadline of twelve months. As time went by, the project manager settled in, and after a couple of weeks, the project manager's boss came to see her. He asked her how many lines of code had been written for the project (please not that this is not too unusual measure for computer programming types). She replied, "Well, none at the moment. We are describing the user's requirements and doing some planning for the project, but no, we have no lines of code written." This seemed to satisfy her boss for the time being, and the project manager continued her work. After about a month, the project manager's boss showed up again and asked the same question, "how many lines of code have you and your project team written?" The project manager, recognizing the concern of her boss, replied, "well, none, but we are getting organized. We have defined our deliverables for the project and we have started our risk analysis, but no, we have no lines of code written. Somewhat shaken the boss left. Well, as you can imagine this went on for some time. The project manager did planning and organizing for the project execution to take place, and her boss got more and more frantic with each passing day. To make a twelve-month long story short, after eleven months, the project was complete. The customer and all the stakeholders were happy. The project was fully tested and met or exceeded the requirements as specified. The customer accepted the system and paid the bill. The project manager's boss decided to throw a party for the entire project team. So, one Friday afternoon, the office was closed and everyone had pizza and beverages. The project manager's boss took the project manager aside during the party and said, "I want to congratulate you on getting this project done within the time required, but it seems to me that if you had not been messing around doing that planning stuff and gotten busy writing code from the start, we would have been done about two months sooner."

This is the kind of reward you can expect when you are trying to follow good project-management practices and you are working in an environment where such practices are new to the management of your organization. Sometimes a little training in the ways and methods of project management is in order. Often we find that companies spend many thousands of dollars on training people who will manage projects and do not train any of the higher level managers. When the project managers try to implement something new that they have learned, they are frequently frustrated by upper management's resistance to change.

Sometimes it seems that getting these executive managers into some sort of project management course is more work than it's worth. But it is imperative that we do so, if only so that they will appreciate and understand some of the things that our new project managers are trying to do.

Advantages of Project Management

Project management brings together the tools and techniques that are needed to make projects successful. But, what do we mean by a successful project? A successful project is a project that meets or exceeds the expectations of the stakeholders in the project.

By organizing the project in a way that concentrates the efforts of the project team on accomplishing the project, a great deal of motivation is achieved. This allows the project teams to concentrate on the project and not be as distracted by all of the other projects and business activities that are going on around them.

The stakeholders have consistent points of contact with the project team, and the project manager is a reliable source of information about the project and all that is going on within it.

The tools and techniques of project management are tried and tested techniques that can be used in virtually any project with success. Nearly all of them have been available for many years but have been somewhat difficult to use without the aid of personal computers. Project management brings many of these tools together in one methodology that can be successfully applied.

In project management we frequently speak of the triple constraint of project scope, project budget, and project time. This means that projects must be completed using the budget that was allocated to them in the time that was allocated to them, and that they must meet the stakeholders' expectations.

Project Management Organizations

Organizations can be structured in only three ways. All organizations are derivations or combinations of the following three structures: (1) projectized organization; (2) traditional organization; and (3) matrix organization.

Projectized Organization: The first type of organization was probably the pure project organization. In this type of organization the project manager is the supreme authority, and all questions regarding the project are directed to her/him as the ultimate authority. The project manager makes all of the decisions.

Early organizations were of this type of organization. When the Egyptian pyramids were built, this type of organization was used. The project manager answered directly to the pharaoh, and there were thousands of people dedicated to the completion of the project. The project took place far from the formal organization, and most resources were completely dedicated to the project.

People who work in these kinds of organizations are generally dedicated to the project until it is over. In some early projects, such as building the Egyptian pyramids, people frequently worked on these projects until they were over. This type of project organization is necessary when there is a very large project of great importance at stake or the project is taking place a great distance from the main organization. The relationship between having a good focus on the goals of the project and good motivation is clear, and people respond well to a clear focus.

In this type of organization, the focus of the project team is clear and the project goals are clearly in sight. There is a clear representative to the customer, and communications to the customer and the project team are usually quite good.

There are some serious disadvantages to this kind of organization, however. The first is one of efficiency. If a person with a special skill is needed, this person must be brought to the project for the duration of time that this skill is required, even if the skill is needed only part of the time. A stone carver who specializes in carving birds might be needed for only one week per month, but because of the distance and difficulty transporting this person to and from the project site, this person would have to be employed full time. For the other three weeks of the month this person would have to be utilized in some other capacity.

The second problem with this type of organization is what to do with the workers when the project is over. There were thousands of people working on a pyramid out in the desert. They all had the goal of construction a pyramid. They all had a deadline of getting it done before the pharaoh died. When the pyramid was finished, so was the project and so was the team.

In modern times, the same scenario happens in this type of organization. For example, look at the Apollo program. President John F. Kennedy gave his famous speech and said, "I believe this nation should commit itself to the goal of sending a man to the moon before the end of the decade and returning him safely to Earth." As we all know, this goal was met in July 1969 when Neil Armstrong first stepped on the surface of the moon. At the same time, NASA managers were figuring out what to do now that the program was over. For a time they were able to keep life in the program, but eventually the funding dried up, and many of the highly skilled aerospace engineers and managers were terminated. When NASA, a few years later, tried to start up the space shuttle program, many of these former employees had changed careers and were happy in their occupations.

We can say that this type of organization can be used for special projects that are larger in size and/or remote from their home organization. For most of the projects that we will be involved in, this type of organization has too many serious disadvantages to be used successfully.

Traditional Organization: The traditional organization has been with us for quite some time and has been the dominant form of organization for over a hundred years. The development of "scientific management" by such persons as Fredrick Taylor and Henry Ford led to the extensive use of the concepts of this type of organization, and it is still used very much today. In this concept of organization the intention is to place people into the jobs that they do best, train them to perform even better, and organize the work so that it takes advantage of their skills in the greatest possible way.

This kind of organization is set up primarily on the basis of organizing people with similar skills into the same groupings. These groups of people have a manager that is similarly skilled. In this way the skills are concentrated into pools of workers in such a way that the manager can distribute the work to the workers that are best for a specific job. The manager of this group, being experienced in this type of work, is also an appropriate person to recommend training and career enhancing assignments to each of the members of the group.

In the traditional organization, people became specialists in their jobs and became very good at what they did. This allowed them to become somewhat complacent in what they did. As long as they were continually asked to do things that were familiar and within their area of expertise, they were successful. Companies were the same way as well. They were good at what they did as long as they could keep on doing it over and over again with few changes. Companies like these were not easily changed when market demands and new technology entered their business areas.

Supposed Sally worked for a large automotive company in the 1970s. Her job was to design disc break assemblies for all of the cars that this company made. She was very good at it. In fact, you could say that she was as good as anyone in the business. She was so good at designing disc brakes that she had been employee of the month and received many awards for her design in terms of quality and cost. She had been with the company since leaving college and had progressed through the ranks and gotten regular raises. She received training to help enhance her skills and was allowed to go to a limited number of conferences held for people in her profession. She knew that in a few years she would be the head of a design group and perhaps some day become a manager of a department.

Things changed, and the company decided that it would like to diversify into other businesses. One of these businesses involved a super lightweight vehicle. This vehicle required the design of a disc brake assembly of the lightest weight possible. For Sally this meant that she would have to design the brake assembly using materials that she had never used before. This bothered her, and she delayed starting the task. She had no contact with the customer or the strategic objectives of this project.

Meanwhile, Sally's boss was also less than enthusiastic about the project. Fortunately for him, the new ultra-lightweight vehicle was only a minor part of the work that was going on in his department. As a result, he did not monitor Sally too much on the design of the disc brake assembly. To him it seemed that there was more important work of the company's normal business to take care of. This new, here today and gone tomorrow, super lightweight vehicle was just another dream of the marketing department and not anything to be concerned about when there were thousands of customers continuing to buy the standard products of the company.

In another department of the company, where the bulk of the work was taking place in the vehicle design, the manager there was under a lot of pressure to get this design completed, because it represented a larger amount of the work that must be done in that department. His job was all the more difficult since his fellow department heads, like Sally's boss, were not concerned with this new project. In addition, this manager probably had very little direct contact with the customer, and the communications problem of going through the marketing people and sales people to find out what the customer really wanted was formidable.

As long as companies continue to do the same sort of things that they have always done, this type of organization works well. Each person has a boss who knows what the person's job is and how well the person does it. The boss knows how to administer salaries, training, and all the other administrative things that employees need. His or her familiarity with the work and that of the people doing the work allows the boss to best use the skills of the workers.

The problem with this kind of organization is that it is difficult to make a change in what people do. Sally avoided working on the ultra-lightweight vehicle because it was more difficult for her to have to learn new things to get the job done. She was being measured by the number of designs she completed and, to a less extent, the difficulty of the designs. She naturally avoided the difficult and new in favor of the tried and true. Since the whole company worked this way, it was very resistant to change the development of new products.

Matrix Organization: The matrix organization came into the picture in the 1970s. This was an attempt to put the best of the projectized and the traditional organizations together.

In the matrix organization, all of the employees report to functional managers much like the managers in the traditional organization. In the matrix organization, the employees are organized strictly by skills. In the traditional organization, there are many exceptions to organizing by skills. An electrical engineer might be in a department of mechanical engineering, for example. In matrix organizations, this does not take place. All people with the same skill report to the same functional manager. The functional managers are responsible for project managers' staffing and direct the administrative work that is needed for the employees. The project managers direct the bulk of the work done by the employees.

There is an organization of project managers as well. The project managers are responsible for the work that is done by the individuals who are assigned to do them. The project managers are not responsible for the administrative work that must be done for the employees. This allows the project managers to form teams that can concentrate on the project at hand and not bogged down by administrative work. It allows the project team to focus on the customer, the stakeholders, and the project, much like the projectized organization.

In operation, the project manager puts together the project plans and develops a need for people to work on them. He or she then meets with the functional manager and negotiates for the people that are available and have the proper skills to work on the project. Together they develop the staff that will work on the project. The functional managers do this with all of the project managers that require skills that are in their organizations. The project managers then meet with the functional managers who have employees that are needed for the project.

One way of thinking about this is: if a project manager has a Gantt chart that lists all of the activities in a project, the functional manager has a similar chart showing all of the employees in the organization and the projects that they are assigned to work on as bars against timeline.

There are several difficulties with this kind of organization. There needs to be a balance of power between the project managers and the functional managers to allocate the best people to their projects and sometimes even more people than necessary. The result of this is that all of the people report to project managers and the project managers trade people between projects without consulting with the functional manager. The functional managers end up being underutilized. This type of organization where the project manager is very powerful is called a strong matrix organization.

If the balance of power is toward the functional managers, then we end up with the old traditional organization, only now we have a group of project managers as well. Sooner or later someone will realize that the functional managers are assigning and monitoring all of the work, and the project managers are merely expediting projects. The type of organization where the project manager has less power than the functional manager is called a weak matrix organization.

Balance can be achieved by deciding when work should be done by the project team and when work should be assigned to the functional department organizations themselves. Make the decision that any work in a project that requires a person to work full time for more than one month will be done under the direction of the project manager, and any work that takes less time than this will be assigned to the functional organization. This allows work to be done in the functional areas as well as in the projects. The type of organization where there is a balance of power between the functional managers and the project managers is called a balanced matrix organization.

PMP Certification Process

The Project Management Professional (PMP) certification exam is administered by the Project Management Institute (PMI). This certification program was developed to prove one's ability to manage projects. Worldwide, there are over 27,000 Project Management Professionals (PMP).

The PMP Program supports the international community of project management professionals and is designed to objectively assess and measure professional knowledge. PMP program requirements and eligibility standards are applied fairly, impartially, and consistently with applicable laws. The PMP program complies with all USA state and federal government nondiscriminatory statutes and laws, and grants certification independently of a candidate's membership or non-membership in any organization, association or other group.

To achieve PMP certification, each candidate must satisfy all educational and experiential requirements established by PMI and must demonstrate an acceptable and valid level of understanding and knowledge of project management that is tested by the PMP Certification Examination. In addition, those who have been granted PMP credential must demonstrate ongoing professional commitment to the field of project management by satisfying Professional Development Program requirements.

Certification Program Mission

The PMI Certification Program delivers world-class project management products and services to support reliance on the Project Management Professional (PMP) certification globally, in both the public and private sectors.

1

PROJECT MANAGEMENT FRAMEWORK

What is a Project?
Project Phases
General Management Skills
Project Processes

What is a Project?

Organizations perform work. Work generally involves either operations or projects, although the two may overlap sometimes. Operations and projects share many characteristics; for example, they are performed by people; constrained by limited resource; and, planned, executed and controlled.

Projects are often implemented as a means of achieving an organization's strategic plan. Operations and projects differ primarily in that operations are ongoing and repetitive while projects are temporary and unique. A project can thus be defined in terms of its distinctive characteristics—*a project is a temporary endeavor undertaken to create a unique product or service. Temporary* means that every project has a definite beginning and a definite end. *Unique* means that the product or service is different in some distinguishing way from all other products or services. For many organizations, projects are a means to respond to those requests that cannot be addressed within the organization's normal operational limits.

Projects are undertaken at all levels of the organization. They may involve a single person or many thousands. Their duration ranges from a few days to more than five years. Projects may involve a single unit of one organization or may cross organizational boundaries, as in joint ventures and partnering. Projects are critical to the realization of the performing organization's business strategy because projects are a means by which strategy is implemented. Examples of projects include:

- Developing or acquiring a new or modified information system;
- Developing a new product or service;
- Designing a new vehicle, plane or other means of transportation;
- Running a campaign for political offices;
- Constructing a building or facility;
- Implementing a new business procedure or process.

Now, let us look at the definitions of some of the words used in the *Guide to the PMBOK*:

Temporary: Temporary means that every project has a definite beginning and a definite end. The end is reached when the project's objectives have been achieved, or when it becomes clear that the project objectives will not or cannot be met, or the need for the project no longer exists and the project is terminated. Temporary does not necessarily mean short in duration; many projects last for several years. In every case, however, the duration of a project is finite; projects are not ongoing efforts.

In addition, temporary does not generally apply to the product or service created by the project. Projects may often have intended and unintended social, economic, and environmental impacts that far outlast the projects themselves. Most project are undertaken to create a lasting result. For example, a project to erect a national monument will create a result expected to last for centuries. A series of projects and/or complementary projects in parallel may be required to achieve a strategic objective.

The objectives of projects and operations are fundamentally different. The objective of a project is to attain the objective and close the project. The objective of an ongoing nonprojectized operation is normally to sustain the business. Projects are fundamentally different because the project ceases when its declared objectives have been attained, while nonproject undertakings adopt a new set of objectives and continue to work.

Unique: Project involve doing something that has not been done before and which is, therefore, *unique*. A product or service may be unique even if the category to which it belongs is large. For example, many thousands of office buildings have been developed, but each individual facility is unique—different owner, different design, different location, different contractor, etc. The presence of respective elements does not change the fundamental uniqueness of the project work. For example, a project to develop a new commercial airliner may require multiple prototypes; a project to bring a new drug to market may require thousands of doses of the drug to support clinical trials; or a real estate development project may include hundreds of individual units.

Progressive Elaboration: Progressive elaboration is a characteristic of projects that integrates the concepts of temporary and unique. Because the product of each project is unique, the characteristics that distinguish the product or service must be progressively elaborated. *Progressively* means "proceeding in steps; continuing steadily by increments," while *elaboration* means "worked out with care and detail; developed thoroughly." These distinguishing characteristics will be broadly defined early in the project, and will be made more explicit and detailed as the project team develops a better and more complete understanding of the product.

Progressive elaboration of product characteristics must be carefully coordinated with proper project scope definition, particularly if the project is performed under contract. When properly defined, the scope of the project—the work to be done—should remain constant even as the product characteristics are progressively elaborated. The relationship between product scope and project scope is discussed further in Chapter 5.

The following example illustrates progressive elaboration:

The product of an economic development project may initially be defined as: "Improve the quality of life of the lowest income residents of community X." As the project proceeds, the products may be described more specifically as, for example: "Provide access to food and water to 1,000 low-income residents in community X." The next round of progressive elaboration might focus exclusively on increasing agriculture production and marketing, with provision of water deemed to be secondary priority to be initiated once the agriculture component is well under way.

Project Phases

Because projects are unique undertakings, they involve a degree of uncertainty. Organizations performing projects will usually divide each project into several *project phases* to improve management control and provide for links to the ongoing operations of the performing organization. Collectively, the project phases are known as the *project life cycle*.

Characteristics of Project Phases: Each project phase is marked by completion of one or more deliverables. A *deliverable* is a tangible, verifiable work product such as a feasibility study, a detail design, or a working prototype. The deliverables, and hence the phases, are part of a generally sequential logic designed to ensure proper definition of the product of the project.

The conclusion of a project phase is generally marked by a review of both key deliverables and project performance to date, to (1) determine if the project should continue into its next phase, and (2) detect and correct errors cost effectively. These phase-end reviews are often called *phase exits*, *kill points*, or *stage gates*.

Each project phase normally includes a set of defined deliverables designed to establish the desired level of management control. The majority of these items are related to the primary phase deliverables, and the phases typically take their names from these items; requirements, design, build, test, startup, turnover, and others, as appropriate.

Characteristics of the Project Life Cycles: The project life cycle serves to define the beginning and the end of a project. For example, when as organization identifies an opportunity to which it would like to respond, it will often authorize a needs assessment and/or a feasibility study to decide if it should undertake a project. The project life-cycle definition will determine whether the feasibility study is treated as the first project phase or as a separate, standalone project.

The project life-cycle definition will also determine which traditional actions at the beginning and the end of the project are included and which are not. In this manner, the project life-cycle definition can be used to link the project to the ongoing operations of the performing organization.

The phase sequence defined by most project life cycles generally involves some form of technology transfer or handoff such as requirements to design, construction to operations, or design to manufacturing. Deliverables from the preceding phase are usually approved before work starts on the next phase. However, a subsequent phase sometimes begun prior to approval of the previous phase deliverables when the risks involved are deemed acceptable. This practice of overlapping phases is often called *fast tracking*.

Project life cycles generally define the followings:

- What technical work should be done in each phase (e.g., is the work of the architect part of the definition phase or part of the execution phase?);
- Who should be involved in each phase (e.g., implementers who need to be involved with requirements and design.)

Project life-cycle descriptions may be very general or very detailed. Highly detailed descriptions may have numerous forms, charts, and checklists to provide structure and consistency. Such detailed approaches are often called *project management methodologies*.

Most project life-cycle descriptions share a number of common characteristics, as described bellow:

- Cost and staffing levels are low at the start, higher toward the end, and drop rapidly as the project draws to a conclusion. This pattern is illustrated below:

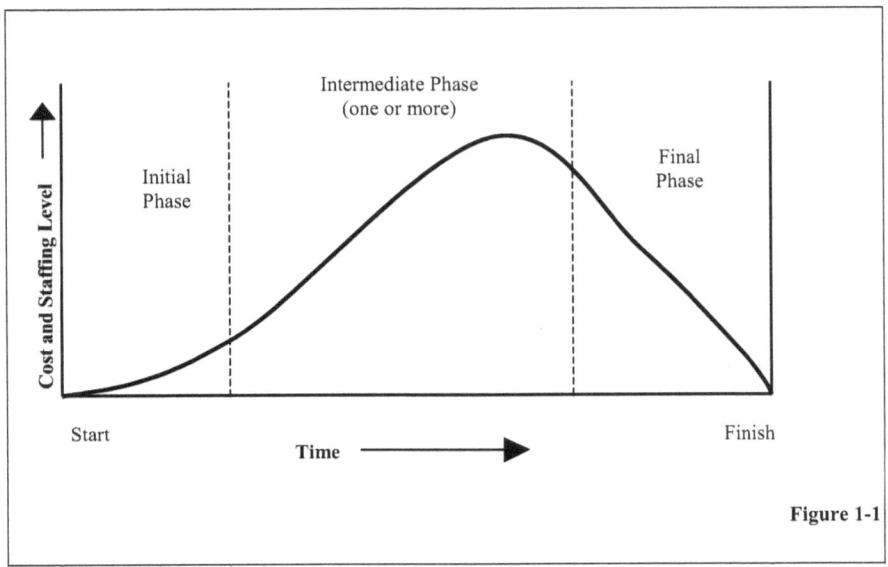

Figure 1-1

- The probability of successfully completing the project is lowest, and hence risk and uncertainty are highest, at the start of the project. The probability of successful completion generally gets progressively higher as the project continues.

- The ability of the stakeholders to influence the final characteristics of the project's product and the final cost of the project is highest at the start and gets progressively lower as the project continues. A major contributor to this phenomenon is that the cost of changes and error correction generally increases as the project continues.

Care should be taken to distinguish the *project* life cycle from the *product* life cycle. For example, a project undertaken to bring a new desktop computer to market is but one phase or stage of the product life cycle.

Although many project life cycles have similar phase names with similar deliverables required, few are identical. Most have four or five phases, but some have nine or more. Even within a single application area, there can be significant variations—one organization's software development life cycle may have a single design phase while another's has separate phases for functional and detail design.

Subprojects within projects may also have distinct project life cycles. For example, an architectural firm hired to design a new office building is first involved in the owner's definition phase when doing the design, and in the owner's implementation phase when supporting the construction effort. The architect's design project, however, will have its own series of phases from conceptual development through definition and implementation to closure. The architect may even treat designing the facility and supporting the construction as separate projects with their own distinct phases.

Representative Project Life Cycles: The following project life cycles have been chosen to illustrate the diversity of approaches in use. The examples shown are typical; they are neither recommended nor preferred. In each case, the phase names and major deliverables are those described by the author of each of the figures.

Defense acquisition: The United States Department of Defense Instruction 5000.2 in Final Coordination Draft, April 2000, describes a series of acquisition milestones and phases as illustrated below:

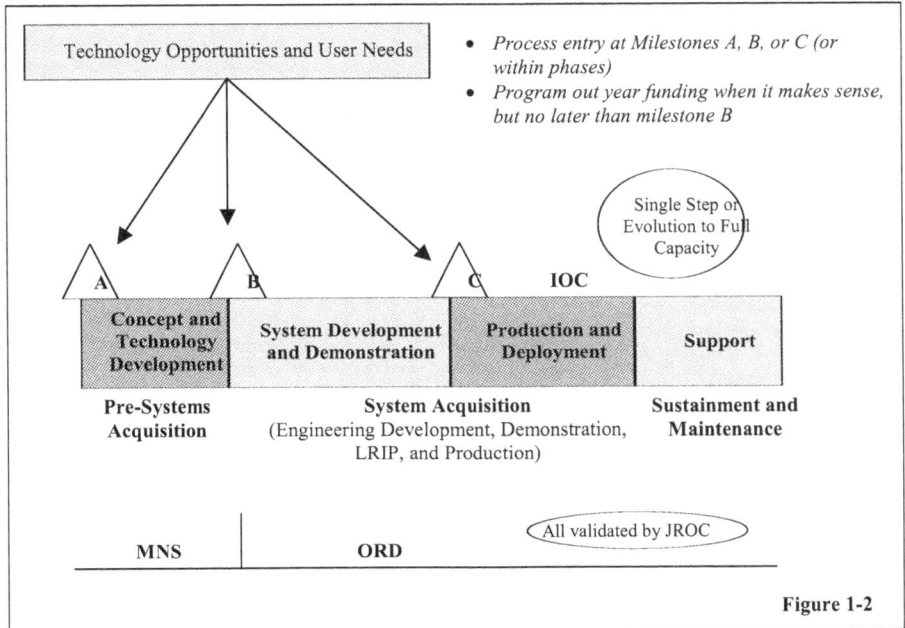

Figure 1-2

- Concept and technology development—paper studies of alternative concept/technology demonstration of new system concepts. Ends with selection of a system architecture and a mature technology to be used.

- System development and demonstration—system integration; risk reduction; demonstration of engineering development models; development and early operational test and evaluation. Ends with system demonstration in an operational environment.

- Production and deployment—low rate initial production (LRIP); complete development of manufacturing capability; phase overlaps with ongoing operations and support.

- Support—this phase is part of the *product* life cycle, but is really ongoing management. Various *projects* may be conducted during this phase to improve capability, correct defects, etc.

Construction: Adapted by Morris, describes a construction project life cycle, as illustrated bellow:

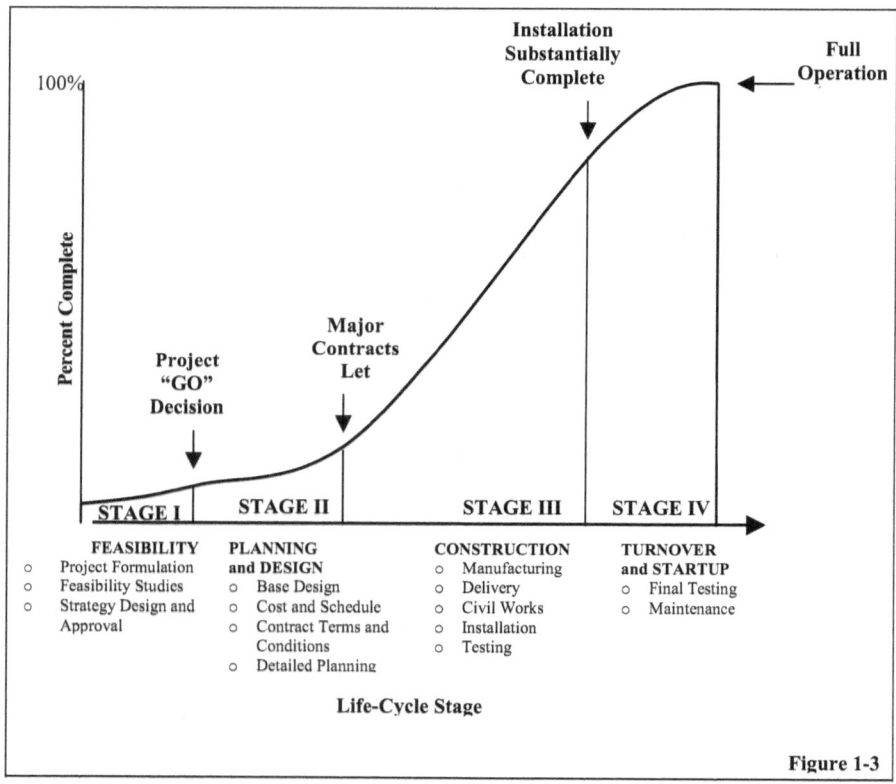

Figure 1-3

- Feasibility—project formulation, feasibility studies, and strategy design and approval. A go/no-go decision is made at the end of this phase.

- Planning and design—base design, cost and schedule, contract terms and conditions, and detailed planning. Major contracts are let at the end of this phase.

- Construction—manufacturing, delivery, civil works, installation, and testing. The facility is substantially complete at the end of this phase.

- Turnover and startup—final testing and maintenance. The facility is in full operation at the end of this phase.

Pharmaceuticals: Murphy describes a project life cycle for pharmaceutical new development in the United States, as illustrated bellow:

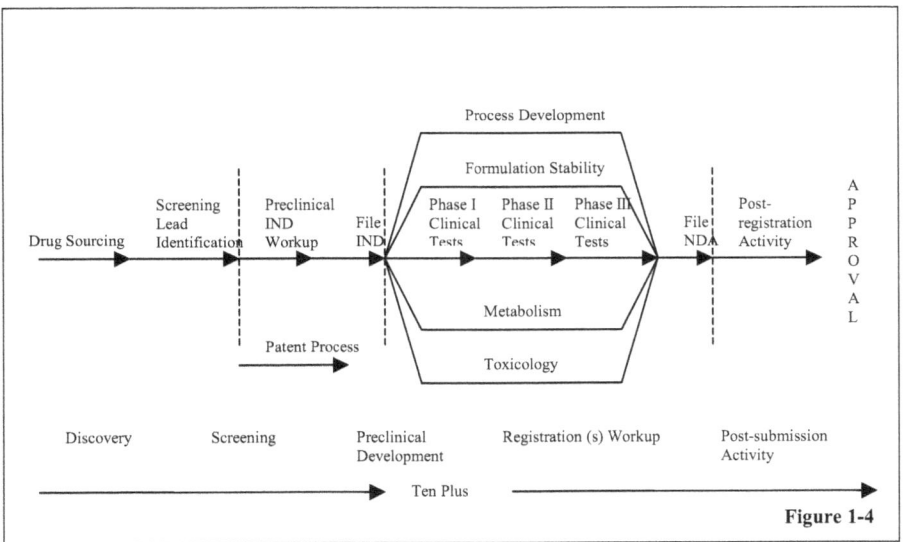

Figure 1-4

- Discovery and screening—includes basic and applied research to identify candidates for preclinical testing.
- Preclinical development—includes laboratory and animal testing to determine safety and efficacy, as well as preparation and filing of an Investigation New Drug (IND) application.
- Registration(s) workup—includes Clinical Phases I, II, and III tests, as well as preparation and filing of a New Drug Application (NDA).
- Post-submission activity—includes additional work as required to support Food and Drug Administration review of the NDA.

General Management Skills

General management is a broad subject dealing with every aspect of managing an ongoing enterprise. Among other topics, it includes:

➢ Finance and accounting, sales and marketing, research and development, and manufacturing and distribution.

➢ Strategic planning, tactical planning, and operational planning.

➢ Organizational structures, organizational behavior, personnel administration, compensation, benefits, and career paths.

➢ Managing oneself through personal time management, stress management, and other techniques.

General management skills provide much of the foundation for building project management skills. They are often essential for the project manager. On any given project, skill in any number of general management areas may be required. This section describes key general management skills that are most likely to affect most projects and that are not covered elsewhere in this manual.

These skills are well documented in the general management literature, and their application is fundamentally the same on a project.

There are also many general management skills that are relevant only on certain projects or in certain application areas. For example, team member safety is critical on virtually all construction projects and of little concern on most software development projects.

Communicating: Communication involves the exchange of information. The sender is responsible for making the information clear, unambiguous, and complete so that the receiver can receive it correctly. The receiver is responsible for making sure that the information is received in its entirety and understood correctly. Communicating has many dimensions:

• Written and oral, listening and speaking.

- Internal (within the project) and external (to the customer, the media, the public, etc.).
- Formal (reports, briefings, etc.) and informal (memos, ad hoc conversations, etc.).
- Vertical (up and down the organization) and horizontal (with peers and partner organization).

The general management skill of communicating is related to, but not the same as, Project Communications Management (described in Chapter 7). Communicating is the broader subject and involves a substantial body of knowledge that is not unique to the project context, for example:

o Sender-receiver models—feedback loops, barriers to communications, etc.

o Choice of media—when to communicate in writing, when to communicate orally, when to write an informal memo, when to write a formal report, etc.

o Writing style—active versus passive voice, sentence structure, word choice, etc.

o Presentation techniques—body language, design of visual aids, etc.

o Meeting management techniques—preparing an agenda, dealing with conflict, etc.

Project Communications Management is the application of these broad concepts to the specific needs of a project—for example, deciding how, when, in what form, and to whom to report project performance.

Leading: Kotter distinguishes between *leading* and *managing* while emphasizing the need for both: one without the other is likely to produce poor results. He says that managing is primarily concerned with "consistently producing key results expected by stakeholders," while leading involves:

- Establishing direction—developing both a vision of the future and strategies for producing the changes needed to achieve that vision.

- Aligning people—communication the vision by words and deeds to all whose cooperation may be needed to achieve the vision.
- Motivating and inspiring—helping people energize themselves to overcome political, bureaucratic, and resource barriers to change.

On a project, particularly a larger project, the project manager is generally expected to be the project's leader as well. Leadership is not, however, limited to the project manager: it may be demonstrated by many different individuals at many times during the project. Leadership must be demonstrated at all levels of the project (project leadership, technical leadership, and team leadership).

Problem Solving: This involves a combination of problem definition and decision-making. *Problem definition* requires distinguishing between causes and symptoms. Problems may be internal (a key employee is reassigned to another project) or external (a permit required to begin work is delayed). Problems may be technical (differences of opinion about the best way to design a product), managerial (a functional group is not producing according to plan), or interpersonal (personality or style clashes).

Decision-making includes analyzing the problem to identify viable solutions, and then making a choice from among them. Decisions can be made or obtained (from the customer, from the team, or from a functional manager). Once made, decisions must be implemented. Decisions also have a time element to them—the "right" decision may not be the "best" decision if it is made too early or too late.

Negotiating: This involves conferring with others to come to terms with them or reach an agreement. Agreements may be negotiated directly or with assistance; mediation and arbitration are two types of assisted negotiation.

Negotiations occur around many issues, at many times, and at many levels of the project. During the course of a typical project, project staff is likely to negotiate for any or all of the following:

- Scope, cost, and schedule objectives;

- Changes to scope, cost, or schedule;
- Contract terms and conditions;
- Assignments;
- Resources.

Influencing the Organization: Influencing the organization involves the ability to "get things done." It requires an understanding of both the formal and informal structures of all organizations involved—the performing organization, customer, partners, contractors, and numerous others, as appropriate. Influencing the organization also requires an understanding of the mechanics of power and politics.

Both power and politics are used here in their positive sense. Pfeffer defines power as "the potential ability to influence behavior, to change the course of events, to overcome resistance, and to get people to do things that they would not otherwise do." In similar fashion, Eccles et al. say that "politics is about getting collective action from a group of people who may have quite different interests. It is about being willing to use conflict and disorder creatively. The negative sense, of course, derives from the fact that attempts to reconcile these interests result in power struggles and organizational games that can sometimes take on a thoroughly unproductive life of their own."

Project Processes

Projects are composed of processes. A *process* is "a series of actions bringing about a result". Project processes are performed by people and generally fall into one of the following two major categories:

- *Project management processes* describe, organize, and complete work of the project. The project management processes that are applicable to most projects, most of the time, are described briefly in following chapters of this manual.

- *Product-oriented processes* specify and create the project's product. Product-oriented processes are typically defined by the project life cycle and vary by application area.

Project management processes and product-oriented processes overlap and interact throughout the project. For example, the scope of the project cannot be defined in the absence of some basic understanding of how to create the product.

Process Groups: Project management processes can be organized into five groups of one or more processes each:

- Initiating processes—authorizing the project or phase;
- Planning processes—defining and refining objectives and selecting the best of the alternative courses of action to attain the objectives that the project was undertaken to address;
- Executing processes—coordinating people and other resources to carry out the projected plan;
- Controlling processes—ensuring that project objectives are met by monitoring and measuring progress regularly to identify variances from plan so that corrective actions can be taken whenever necessary;
- Closing processes—formalizing acceptance of the project or phase and bringing it to an orderly end.

The process groups are linked by the results they produce—the result or outcome of one often becomes an input to another. Among the central process groups, the links are iterated—planning provides executing with a documented project plan early on, and then provides documented updates to the plan as the project progresses. These connections are illustrated below:

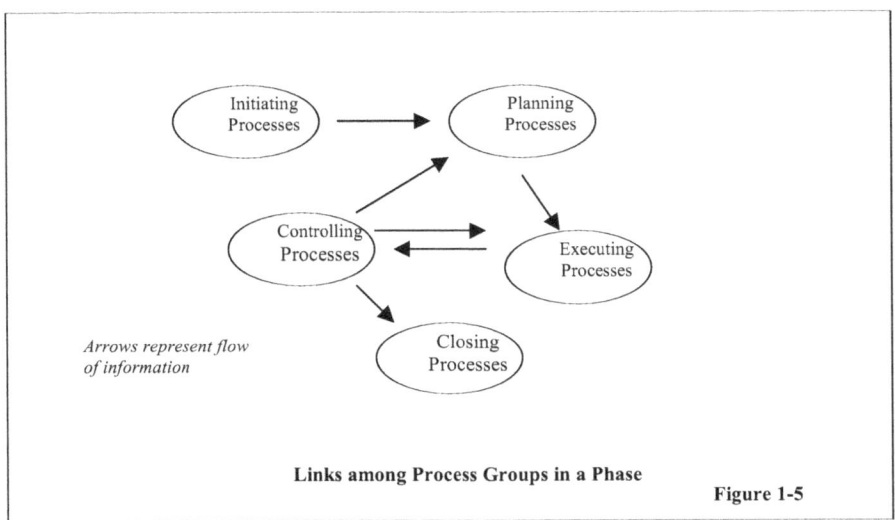

Links among Process Groups in a Phase

Figure 1-5

Additionally, the project management process groups are not discrete, on-time events; they are overlapping activities that occur at varying levels of intensity throughout each phase of the project. The chart below illustrates how the process groups overlap and vary within a phase:

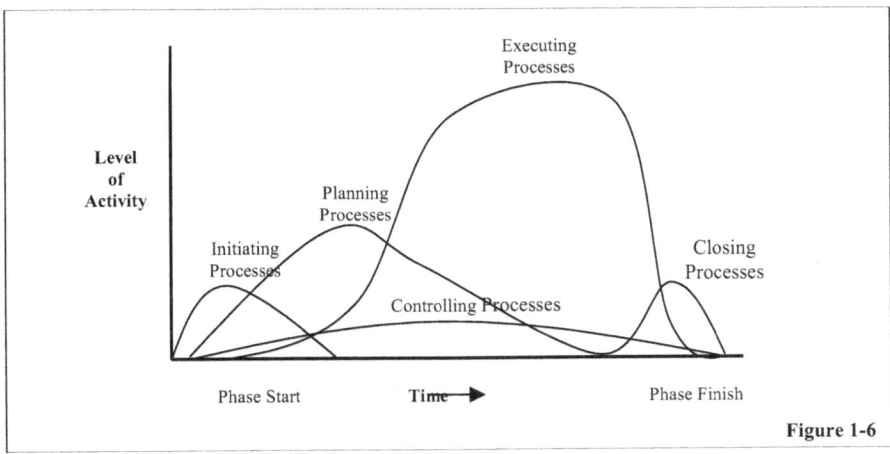

Figure 1-6

Finally, the process group interactions also cross phases such that closing one phase provides an input to initiating the next. For example, closing a design phase requires customer acceptance of the design document. Simultaneously, the design document defines the product description for the ensuing implementation phase.

Repeating the initiation processes at the start of each phase helps to keep the project focused on the business need that it was undertaken to address. It should also help ensure that the project is halted if the business need no longer exists, or if the project is unlikely to satisfy that need. Business needs are discussed in more detail in Chapter 4 of this manual.

It is important to note that the actual inputs and outputs of the processes depend heavily upon the phase in which they are carried out. The planning process, for example, must not only provide details of the work to be done to bring the current phase of the project to successful completion, but must also provide some preliminary description of work to be done in later phases. This progressive detailing of the project plan is often called *rolling wave planning*, indicating that planning is an iterative and ongoing process.

Involving stakeholders in the project phases generally improves the probability of satisfying customer requirements and realizes the *buy-in* or shared ownership of the project by the stakeholders, which is often critical to project success.

Process Interactions: Within each process group, the individual processes are linked by their inputs and outputs. By focusing on these links, one can describe each process in terms of its:

- Inputs—documents or documentable items that will be acted upon;
- Tools and Techniques—mechanisms applied to the inputs to create the outputs;
- Outputs—documents or documentable items that are results of the process.

Initiating Processes

o Initiation—authorizing the project or phase is part of project scope management.

Planning Processes

Planning is of major importance to a project because the project involves doing something that has not been done before. As a result, there are relatively more processes in this section. However, the number of processes does not mean that project management is primarily planning—the amount of planning performed should be commensurate with the scope of the project and the usefulness of the information developed. Planning is an ongoing effort throughout the life of the project.

Core processes: Some planning processes have clear dependencies that require them to be performed in essentially the same order on most projects. For example, activities must be defined before they can be scheduled or costed. These *core planning processes* may be iterated several times during any one phase of a project. They include the following:

o Scope Planning—developing a written scope statement as the basis for future project decisions.

o Scope Definition—subdividing the major project deliverables into smaller, more manageable components.

o Activity Definition—identifying the specific activities that must be performed to produce the various project deliverables.

o Activity Sequencing—identifying and documenting interactivity dependencies.

o Activity Duration Estimating—estimating the number of work periods that will be needed to complete individual activities.

o Schedule Development—analyzing activity sequences, activity durations, and resource requirements to create the project schedule.

o Resources Planning—determining what resources (people, equipment, materials, etc.) and what quantities of each should be used to perform project activities.

o Risk Management Planning—deciding how to approach and plan for risk management in a project.

o Cost estimating—developing an approximation (estimate) of the costs of the resources required to complete project activities.

o Cost budgeting—allocating the overall cost estimate to individual work packages.

o Project Plan Development—taking the results of other planning processes and putting them into a consistent, coherent document.

Facilitating processes: Interactions among the other planning processes are more dependent on the nature of the project. For example, on some projects, there may be little or no identifiable risk until after most of the planning has been done and the team recognizes that the cost and schedule targets are extremely aggressive and thus involve considerable risk. Although these *facilitating processes* are performed intermittently and as needed during project planning, they are not optional. They include the following:

o Quality Planning—identifying which quality standards are relevant to the project and determining how to satisfy them.

o Organizational Planning—identifying, documenting, and assigning project roles, responsibilities, and reporting relationships.

o Staff Acquisition—getting the human resources needed assigned to and working on the project.

o Communications Planning—determining the information and communications needs of the stakeholders: who needs what information, when will they need it, and how will it be given to them.

o Risk Identification—determining which risks are likely to affect the project and documenting the characteristics of each.

o Qualitative Risk Analysis—performing a qualitative analysis of risks and conditions to prioritize their effects on project objectives.

o Quantitative Risk Analysis—measuring the probability and impact of risks and estimating their implications for project objectives.

o Risk Response Planning—developing procedures and techniques to enhance opportunities and to reduce threats to the project's objectives from risk.

o Procurement Planning—determining what to procure, how much to procure, and when.

o Solicitation Planning—documenting product requirements and identifying potential sources.

Executing Processes

The executing processes include core processes and facilitating processes. It includes the following:

o Project Plan Execution—carrying out the project plan by performing the activities included therein.

o Quality Assurance—evaluating overall project performance on a regular basis to provide confidence that the project will satisfy the relevant quality standards.

o Team Development—developing individual and group skills/competencies to enhance project performance.

o Information Distribution—making needed information available to project stakeholders in a timely manner.

o Solicitation—obtaining quotations, bids, offers, or proposals as appropriate.

o Source Selection—choosing from among potential sellers.

o Contract Administration—managing the relationship with the seller.

Controlling Processes

Project performance must be monitored and measured regularly to identify variances from the plan. Variances are fed into the control processes in the various knowledge areas. To the extent that significant variances are observed (i.e., those that jeopardize the project objectives), adjustments to the plan are made by repeating the appropriate project planning process. For example, a missed activity finish date may require adjustments to the current staffing plan, reliance on overtime, or tradeoffs between budget and schedule objectives. Controlling also includes taking preventive action in anticipation of possible problems.

The controlling process group contains core processes and facilitating processes, which include the following:

o Integrated Change Control—coordinating changes across the entire project.

o Scope Verification—formalizing acceptance of the project scope.

o Scope Change Control—controlling changes to project scope.

o Schedule Control—controlling changes to the project schedule.

o Cost Control—controlling changes to the project budget.

o Quality Control—monitoring specific project results to determine if they comply with relevant quality standards and identifying ways to eliminate causes of unsatisfactory performance.

o Performance Reporting—collecting and disseminating performance information. This includes status reporting, progress measurement, and forecasting.

o Risk Monitoring and Control—keeping track of identified risks, monitoring residual risks and identifying new risks, ensuring the execution of risk plans, and evaluating their effectiveness in reducing risk.

Closing Processes

Following are the interaction of the core processes:

o Contract Closeout—completion and settlement of the contract, including resolution of any open items.

o Administrative Closure—generating, gathering, and disseminating information to formalize phases or project completion, including evaluating the project and compiling lessons learned for use in planning future projects or phases.

Customizing Process Interactions

The processes and interactions in the above sections meet the test of general acceptance—they apply to most projects most of the time. However, not all of the processes will be needed on all projects, and not all of the interactions will apply to all projects. For example,

- An organization that makes extensive use of contractors may explicitly describe where in the planning process each procurement process occurs.

- The absence of a process does not mean that it should not be performed. The project management team should identify and manage all the processes that are needed to ensure a successful project.

- Projects that are dependent on unique, such as commercial software development, biopharmaceuticals, etc., may define roles and responsibilities prior to scope definition, since what can be done may be a function of who will be available to do it.

- Some process outputs may be predefined as constraints. For example, management may specify a target completion date, rather than allowing it to be determined by the planning process. An imposed completion date may increase project risk, add cost, and compromise quality.

- Large projects may need relatively more details. For example, risk identification might be further subdivided to focus separately on identifying cost risks, schedule risks, technical risks, and quality risks.

- On subprojects and smaller projects, relatively little effort will be spent on processes whose outputs have been defined at the project level (e.g., a subcontractor may ignore risks explicitly assumed by the prime contractor), or on processes that provide only marginal utility (e.g., there may be no formal communications plan on a five-person project).

Mapping of Project Management Processes

The following chart reflects the mapping of the thirty-nine (39) project management processes to the five project management process groups of initiating, planning, executing, controlling, and closing and the nine project management knowledge areas, based on the *PM BOK*. However, please note that this diagram is not meant to be exclusive, but to indicate generally where the project management processes fit into both the project management process groups as well as the project management knowledge areas.

Process Groups / Knowledge Area	Initiating	Planning	Executing	Controlling	Closing
Project Integration Management		Project Plan Development	Project Plan Execution	Integrated Change Control	
Project Scope Management	Initiation	Scope Planning Scope Definition		Scope Verification Scope Change Control	
Project Time Management		Activity Definition Activity Sequencing Activity Duration Estimating Schedule Development		Schedule Control	
Project Cost Management		Resource Planning Cost Estimating Cost Budgeting		Cost Control	
Project Quality Management		Quality Planning	Quality Assurance	Quality Control	
Project Human Resources Management		Organizational Planning Staff Acquisition	Team Development		
Project Communications Management		Communications Planning	Information Distribution	Performance Reporting	Administrative Closure
Risk Project Management		Risk Management Planning Risk Identification Qualitative Risk Analysis Quantitative Risk Analysis Risk Response Planning		Risk Monitoring	
Project Procurement Management		Procurement Planning Solicitation Planning	Solicitation Source Selection Contract Administration		Contract Closure

Mapping of Project Management Processes to the Process Groups and Knowledge Areas

Figure 1-7

2

INTEGRATION MANAGEMENT

Project Planning (includes Plan Development & Execution)
Integrated Change Control

Integration Management

Integration Management includes the processes required to ensure that the various elements of the project are properly coordinated. It involves making tradeoffs among competing objectives and alternatives to meet or exceed stakeholder needs and expectations. While all project management processes are integrative to some degree, the processes described in this chapter are *primarily* integrative. The following chart provides an overview of the major processes:

- *Project Plan Development:* integration and coordinating all project plans to create a consistent, coherent document.

- Project Plan Execution: carrying out the project plan by performing the activities included therein.

- Integrated Change Control: coordinating changes across the entire project.

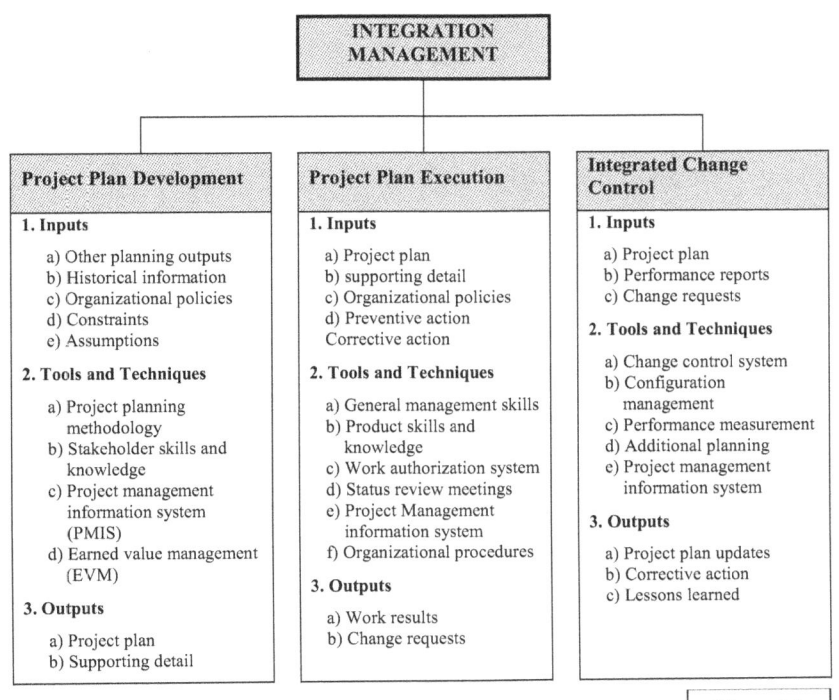

Figure 2-1

Project Plan Development

Project plan development uses the outputs of the other planning processes, including strategic planning, to create a consistent, coherent document that can be used to guide both project execution and project control. This process is almost always iterated several times. For example, the initial draft may include generic resource requirements and an undated sequence of activities while the subsequent versions of the plan will include specific resources and explicit dates. The project scope of work is an iterative process that is generally done by the project team with the use of a Work Breakdown Structure (WBS), allowing the team to capture and then decompose all of the work of the project. All of the defined work must be planned, estimated and scheduled, and authorized with the use of detailed integrated management control plans sometimes called *Control Account Plans*, or CAP's in the Earned Value Management (EVM) process. The sum of all the integrated management control plans will constitute the total project scope.

The project plan is used to:

- Guide project execution;
- Document project planning assumptions;
- Document project planning decisions regarding alternatives chosen;
- Facilitate communication among stakeholders;
- Define key management reviews as to content, extent, and timing;
- Provide a baseline for progress measurement and project control.

Inputs to Project Plan Development

a) *Other planning outputs:* All of the outputs of the planning processes in the other knowledge areas, which were discussed in Chapter 2, are inputs to developing the project plan. Other planning outputs include both base documents, such as Work Breakdown Structure (WBS), and the supporting detail. Many projects will also require application area-specific inputs (e.g., most major projects will require a cash-flow forecast).

b) *Historical information:* The available historical information (e.g. estimating database, records of past project performance) should have been consulted during the other project planning processes. This information should also be available during project plan development to assist with verifying assumptions and assessing alternatives that are identified as part of this process.

c) *Organizational policies:* Any and all of the organizations involved in the project may have formal and informal policies whose effects must be considered. Organizational policies that typically must be considered include, but not limited to the following:

- Quality management—process audits, continuous improvement targets.
- Personnel administration—hiring and firing guidelines, employee performance reviews.
- Financial controls—time reporting, required expenditure and disbursement reviews, accounting codes, standard contract provisions.

d) *Constraints:* A constraint is an applicable restriction that will affect the performance of the project. For example, a predefined budget is a constraint that is highly likely to limit the team's options regarding scope, staffing, and schedule. When a project is performed under contract, contractual provisions will generally be constraints.

e) *Assumptions:* Assumptions are factors that, for planning purposes, are considered to be true, real, or certain. Assumptions affect all aspects of project planning, and are part of the progressive elaboration of the project. Project teams frequently identify, document, and validate assumptions as part of their planning process. For example, if the date that a key person will become available is uncertain, the team may assume a specific start date. Assumptions generally involve a degree of risk.

Tools and Techniques for Project Plan Development

a) *Project Planning Methodology:* A project planning methodology is any structured approach used to guide the project team during development of the project plan. It may be as simple as standard forms and templates (hard copy or electronic, informal or formal) or as complex as a series of required simulations (e.g., Monte Carlo analysis of schedule risk). Most project planning methodologies make use of a combination of "hard" tools, such as project management software, and "soft" tools, such as facilitated startup meetings.

b) Stakeholder Skills and Knowledge: Every stakeholder has skills and knowledge that may be useful in developing the project plan. The project management team must create an environment in which the stakeholders can contribute appropriately. Who contributes, what they contribute, and when they contribute will vary. For example:

- On a project where staffing is defined in advance, the individual contributors may contribute significantly to meeting cost and schedule objectives by reviewing duration and effort estimates for reasonableness.

- On a construction project being done under a lump-sum contract, the professional cost engineer will make a major contribution to the profitability objective during proposal preparation when the contract amount is being determined.

C) *Project Management Information System (PMIS):* A PMIS consists of the tools and techniques used to gather, integrate, and disseminate the outputs of project management processes. It is used to support all aspects of the project from initiating through closing, and can include both manual and automated systems.

D) *Earned Value Management:* A technique used to integrate the project's scope, schedule, and resources and to measure and report project performance from initiation to closeout.

Outputs from Project Plan Development

A) Project Plan: The project plan is a formal, approved document used to manage project execution. The project schedule lists planned dates for performing activities and meeting milestones identified in the project plan. The project plan and schedule should be distributed as defined in the communications management plan (e.g., management of the performing organization may require broad coverage with little detail, while a contractor may require complete details on a single subject). In some application areas, the term *integrated project plan* is used to refer to this document.

A clear distinction should be made between the project plan and the project performance measurement baselines. The project plan is a document or collection of documents that should be expected to change over time as more information becomes available about the project. The performance measurement baseline will usually change only intermittently, and then generally only in response to an approved scope of work or deliverable change.

There are many ways to organize and present the project plan, but it commonly includes all of the following:

- Project charter.
- A description of the project management approach or strategy (a summary of the individual management plans from the other knowledge areas).
- Scope statement, which includes the project objectives and the project deliverables.
- WBS to the level at which control will be exercised, as a baseline scope document.
- Cost estimates, scheduled start and finish dates (schedule), and responsibility assignments for each deliverable within the WBS to the level at which control will be exercised.

- Performance measurement baselines for technical scope, schedule, and cost, i.e., the schedule baseline (project schedule) and the cost baseline (time-phased project budget).
- Major milestones and target dates for each.
- Required (key) staff and their cost and/or effort.
- Risk management plan, including: key risks, constraints and assumptions, and planned responses and contingencies for each.
- Subsidiary management plans, namely:
  o Quality management plan (Chapter 3).
  o Scope management plan (Chapter 4).
  o Cost & Schedule management plan (Chapter 5).
  o Communications management plan (Chapter 6).
  o Risk response plan (Chapter 7).
  o Procurement management plan (Chapter 8).
  o Staffing management plan (chapter 9).
     Each of these plans could be included if needed and with detail to the extent required for each specific project.
- Open issues and pending decisions.

Other project planning outputs should be included in the formal plan, based upon the needs of the individual project. For example, the project plan for a large project will generally include a project organization chart.

B) *Supporting Detail:* Supporting detail for the project plan includes the following:
- Outputs from other planning processes that are not included in the project plan.
- Additional information or documentation generated during development of the project plan (e.g., constraints and assumptions that were not previously known).
- Technical documentation; such as, a history of all requirements, specifications, and conceptual designs.

- Documentation of relevant standards.
- Specifications from early project development planning.

This material should be organized as needed to facilitate its use during project plan execution.

Project Plan Execution

Project plan execution is the primary process for carrying out the project plan—the vast majority of the project's budget will be expended in performing this process. In this process, the project manager and the project management team must coordinate and direct various technical and organizational interfaces that exist in the project. It is the project process that is most directly affected by the project application area in that the product of the project is actually created here. Performance against the project baseline must be continuously monitored so that corrective actions can be taken based on actual performance against the project plan. Periodic forecasts of the final cost and schedule results will be made to support the analysis.

Inputs	Tools & Techniques	Outputs
a) Project plan b) supporting detail c) Organizational policies d) Preventive action Corrective action	a) General management skills b) Product skills and knowledge c) Work authorization system d) Status review meetings e) Project Management information system f) Organizational procedures	a) Work results b) Change requests

Figure 2-2

Inputs to Project Plan Execution

A) Project Plan: The subsidiary management plans (scope management plan, risk management plan, procurement management plan, configuration management plan, etc.) and the performance measurement baselines are key inputs to project plan execution.

B) *Supporting Detail:* Supporting detail for the project plan includes the following:

- Outputs from other planning processes that are not included in the project plan.
- Additional information or documentation generated during development of the project plan (e.g., constraints and assumptions that were not previously known).
- Technical documentation; such as, a history of all requirements, specifications, and conceptual designs.
- Documentation of relevant standards.
- Specifications from early project development planning.

C) *Organizational Policies:* Any and all of the organizations involved in the project may have formal and informal policies that may affect project plan execution.

D) *Preventive Action:* Preventive action is anything that reduces the probability of potential consequences of project risk events.

E) *Corrective Action:* Corrective action is anything done to bring expected future project performance in line with the project plan. Corrective action is an output of the various control processes—as an input here it completes the feedback loop needed to endure effective project management.

Tools and Techniques for Project Plan Execution

A) *General Management Skills:* General management skills such as leadership, communicating, and negotiating are essential to effective project plan execution.

B) *Product Skills and Knowledge:* The project team must have access to an appropriate set of skills and knowledge about the project's product. The necessary skills are defined as part of planning (especially in resource planning, Chapter 8) and are provided through the staff acquisition process (Chapter 9).

C) *Work Authorization System:* A work authorization system is a formal procedure for sanctioning project work to ensure that work is done at the right time and in the proper sequence. The primary mechanism is typically a written authorization to begin work on a specific activity or work package. The design of a work authorization system should balance the value of the control provided with the cost of that control. Fro example, on many smaller projects, verbal authorizations will be adequate.

D) *Status Review Meetings:* Status review meetings are regularly scheduled meetings held to exchange information about the project. On most projects, status review meetings will be held at various frequencies and on different levels (e.g., the project management team may meet weekly by itself and monthly with the customer).

E) *Project Management Information System (PMIS):* A PMIS consists of the tools and techniques used to gather, integrate, and disseminate the outputs of project management processes. It is used to support all aspects of the project from initiating through closing, and can include both manual and automated systems.

F) *Organizational Procedures:* Any and all of the organizations involved in the project may have formal and informal procedures that are useful during project execution.

Outputs from Project Plan Execution

A) *Work Results:* Work results are the outcomes of the activities performed to accomplish the project. Information on work results— which deliverables have been completed and which have not, to what extent quality standards are being met, what costs have been incurred or committed, etc.—is collected as part of project plan execution and fed into the performance reporting process. It should be noted that although outcomes are frequently tangible deliverables such as buildings, roads, etc., they are also often intangibles such as people trained who can effectively apply that training.

B) *Change Requests:* Change requests (e.g., to expand or contract project scope, to modify cost [budgets], or schedule estimates [dates, etc.]) are often identified while the work of the projects is being done.

Integrated Change Control

Integrated change control is concerned with a) influencing the factors that create changes to ensure that changes are agreed upon, b) determining that a change has occurred, and c) managing the actual changes when and as they occur. The original defined project scope and the integrated performance baseline must be maintained by continuously managing changes to the baseline, either by rejecting new changes or by approving changes and incorporating them into a revised project baseline. Integrated change control requires:

- Maintaining the integrity of the performance measurement baseline.

- Ensuring that changes to the product scope are reflected in the definition of the project scope.

- Coordinating changes across knowledge areas. For example, a proposed schedule change will often affect cost, risk, quality, and staffing.

Inputs to Integrated Change Control

A) *Project Plan:* Project plan provides the baseline against which changes will be controlled.

B) *Performance Reports:* Performance reports provide information on project performance. Performance reports may also alert the project team to issues that may cause problems in the future.

C) *Change Requests:* Change requests may occur in many forms—oral or written, direct or indirect, externally or internally initiated, and legally mandated or optional.

Tools and Techniques for Integrated Change Control

A) *Change Control System:* A change control system is a collection of formal, documented procedures that defines how project performance will be monitored and evaluated, and includes the steps by which official project documents may be changed. It includes the paperwork, tracking systems, processes, and approval levels necessary for authorizing changes. In many cases, the performing organization will have a change control system that can be adopted "as is" for use by the project. However, if an appropriate system is not available, the project management team will need to develop one as part of the project.

B) *Configuration Management:* Configuration management is any documented procedure used to apply technical and administrative direction and surveillance to:

- Identify and document the functional and physical characteristics of an item or system.
- Control any changes to such characteristics.
- Record and report the change and its implementation status.

C) *Performance Management:* Performance measurement techniques such as Earned Value (EV) help to assess whether variances form the plan require corrective action.

D) *Additional Planning:* Projects seldom run exactly according to plan. Prospective changes may require new or revised cost estimates, modified activity sequences, schedules, resource requirements, analysis of risk response alternatives, or other adjustments to the project plan.

E) *Project Management Information System (PMIS):* A PMIS consists of the tools and techniques used to gather, integrate, and disseminate the outputs of project management processes. It is used to support all aspects of the project from initiating through closing, and can include both manual and automated systems.

Outputs from Integrated Change Control

A) *Project Plan Updates:* Project plan updates are any modification to the contents of the project plan or the supporting detail. Appropriate stakeholders must be notified as needed.

B) *Corrective Action:* Corrective action is anything done to bring expected future project performance in line with the project plan. Corrective action is an output of the various control processes—as an input here it completes the feedback loop needed to endure effective project management.

C) *Lessons Learned:* The causes of variances, the reasoning behind the corrective action chosen, and other types of lessons learned should be documented so that they become part of the historical database for both this project and other projects of the performing organization. The database is also the basis for knowledge management.

3

QUALITY MANAGEMENT

Quality Planning
Quality Assurance
Cost of Quality
Quality Control
Sampling Inspection and Other Quality Control Techniques

Quality Management

One of the goals of project management is to meet the expectations of the stakeholders of the project. Managing the quality of the project is the function that will allow this to happen. Quality management includes all the work that is necessary to ensure that each of the objectives of the project is met. In the latest edition of the *Guide to the Professional Management Body of Knowledge* (2000), PMI emphasizes that the purpose of the project is to meet the requirements of the stakeholders. In the past, common usage of the project goal was to meet or exceed the customer expectations.

We have discussed methods of controlling the project costs and schedule in the cost and time management chapters. These controls cover only two of the sides of the triple constraint triangle. Quality management controls the third side of the triangle, scope, as well as provides guidance for and assurance of meeting the other two constraints of cost and schedule. It is important to recognize that in modern project management, it is important to meet the stakeholders' expectations.

It is also important that the expectations of the stakeholders are not exceeded. The customer has contracted for certain deliverables, and delivering something that was not asked for can be a waste of time and money. In some cases delivering more than was asked can actually make matters worse.

Quality should not be confused with grade. Quality that is low is always going to be a problem, while a low grade is not necessarily a bad condition. A product may be developed and marketed to appeal to those who want an inexpensive product that will have a limited useful life and function. This product may also have a lower cost. Stakeholders should get what they pay for. The quality of the item means that it is indeed what it intended to be.

The *Guide to the PMBOK* defines three areas of quality management: quality planning, quality assurance, and quality control. It is essential that a distinction be made among these categories.

The quality planning function is the process that determines which quality standards should be used to accomplish the goal of ensuring that the scope of the project fulfills the stakeholders' expectations.

The quality assurance function is a process that monitors the overall ability of the project to meet the expectations of the stakeholders. The purpose of the quality assurance function is to provide the confidence that the project will have the proper controls to be able to meet the standards set forth by the stakeholders at the beginning of the project and documented in the project specifications. The quality assurance function assures that the quality of the project will be sufficient.

The quality control function is the process that is used to measure the specific items that must be monitored and controlled to determine that the project will meet the stakeholders' expectations.

The philosophy of modern quality management is that mistakes should be prevented rather than detected. It is much better to create an environment that prevents mistakes from happening than to spend time and effort trying to detect and deal with problems that have already occurred. Always remember the phrase used to state the idea behind quality management, which is: "You can't inspect quality into a product".

Thus, quality is *"the totality of characteristics of an entity that bear on its ability to satisfy stated or implied needs"*. Stated and implied needs are the inputs to developing project requirements. A critical aspect of quality management in the project context is the necessity to turn implied needs into requirements through project scope management (described in Chapter 4).

The project management team must be careful not to confuse *quality* with *grade*. Grade is "a category or rank given to entities having the same functional use but different technical characteristics". Low quality is always a problem; low grade may not be. For example, a software product may be of high quality (e.g., no obvious bugs, readable manual, etc.) and low grade (e.g., limited number of features, etc.), or of low quality (e.g., many bugs, poorly organized user documentation, etc.) and high grade (e.g., numerous features). Determining and delivering the required levels of both quality and grade are the responsibilities of the project manager and the project management team members.

Quality Planning

The quality planning process must accomplish several things for the project to be successful. There must be an overall quality policy, or company guidelines, for any project. Each project and each interrelated project must modify the guidelines and gain approval on changes that will be required for their particular project.

The result of quality planning process is the quality plan. This plan describes how the quality of the project will be assured and the functions that will be carried out by the project team to accomplish this task. The plan also serves to provide the additional activities that will be added to the project scope, budget, and schedule that will allow these things to happen.

The quality plan should reflect the information that is gathered throughout the project. All of the other areas of the management of the project should complement the quality plan. Risk is of major importance in the quality plan. Areas of the project that are high in risk should have a significant influence on the quality plan.

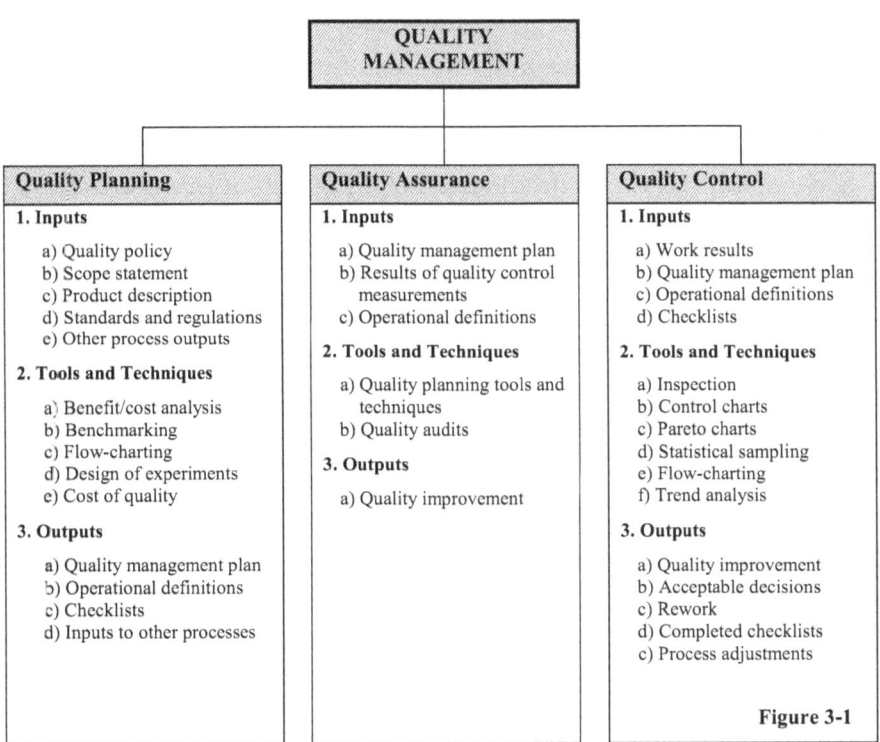

QUALITY MANAGEMENT

Quality Planning

1. Inputs

  a) Quality policy
  b) Scope statement
  c) Product description
  d) Standards and regulations
  e) Other process outputs

2. Tools and Techniques

  a) Benefit/cost analysis
  b) Benchmarking
  c) Flow-charting
  d) Design of experiments
  e) Cost of quality

3. Outputs

  a) Quality management plan
  b) Operational definitions
  c) Checklists
  d) Inputs to other processes

Quality Assurance

1. Inputs

  a) Quality management plan
  b) Results of quality control
     measurements
  c) Operational definitions

2. Tools and Techniques

  a) Quality planning tools and
     techniques
  b) Quality audits

3. Outputs

  a) Quality improvement

Quality Control

1. Inputs

  a) Work results
  b) Quality management plan
  c) Operational definitions
  d) Checklists

2. Tools and Techniques

  a) Inspection
  b) Control charts
  c) Pareto charts
  d) Statistical sampling
  e) Flow-charting
  f) Trend analysis

3. Outputs

  a) Quality improvement
  b) Acceptable decisions
  c) Rework
  d) Completed checklists
  e) Process adjustments

Figure 3-1

Quality Assurance

The *Guide to the PMBOK* defines quality assurance as "all planned and systematic activities implemented within the quality system to provide confidence that the project will satisfy the relevant quality standards".

Quality audits are performed to review certain important areas of the project. Audits make it possible to determine what is happening in the project and whether the project quality is meeting the standards set forth in the quality plan.

The quality assurance function includes the means to continuously improve the quality of future projects as well. Lessons learned from one project are applied to the quality plans of future projects so that there can be an ever-improving level of quality in projects completed by the organization.

Each member of the project team, including each of the stakeholders of the project, is essential to the overall quality assurance of the project. In modern thinking on quality it is the individual person performing work that is really responsible for assuring the quality of the product.

Cost of Quality

As in all things in project management, there should be a favorable ratio of benefits cost to quality (see Figure 3-1). This is usually referred to as prevention rather than cure. The total cost of curing a problem once it has occurred is generally more costly than preventing the problem in the first place. It is apparent that the potential savings between the cost of defects and the cost of prevention are great. Typically, many of the costs of defects are not recognized in an organized way to reflect their true cost. This is because when some of the costs of these defects are recognized, the project has been turned over to a maintenance and support function. The project team may have been dissolved, and the members may be working on other projects. Following is a listing of the considerations for these costs. According to Deming, "Eighty-five percent of the cost of quality [is] the direct responsibility of management."

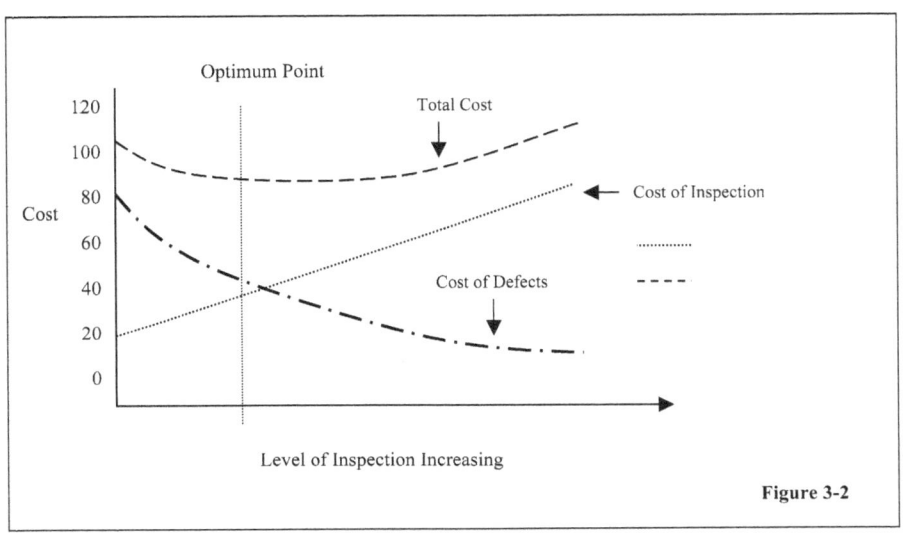

Figure 3-2

Costs of Prevention

 a)   Additional planning.
 b)   Education and training of project team and stakeholders.
 c)   Inspection and testing of the internal and external deliverables of the project.
 d)   Improved designs for quality purposes.
 e)   Quality staff.
 f)   Quality audits.
 g)   Quality plan and execution.

Costs of Defects

 a)   Scrap.
 b)   Rework.
 c)   Repair.
 d)   Replacement of defective parts and inventory.
 e)   Repairs after the delivery of the product(s).
 f)   Loss of future business with the stakeholder.
 g)   Legal issues for nonconformance.

h)   Liability for defect.

i)   Risk to life and property.

Deming's Fourteen Points: Deming is probably best known for his fourteen points on quality. These guidelines were developed during Deming's work with Japanese industries and serve as guideline for the practice of practical quality management (see Figure 3-2).

o Constancy of purpose	o Drive out fear
o Adopt a new philosophy	o Break down barriers
o Eliminate need for inspection	o Eliminate slogans, targets, and the like
o Only consider total cost, not price	o Eliminate management by standards and quotas
o Improve constantly	o Remove barriers to pride of workmanship
o Initiate On Job Training (OJT)	o Institute education and self-improvement
o Initiate leadership	o Get everyone involved

Figure 3-3

Quality Control

The function of quality control is to monitor specific project results to ensure that the results match the standards that were set for the project. The quality control function utilizes a number of techniques to accomplish this task. Many of these tools and techniques are rooted in the concepts of probability and statistics.

Inspection is carried out by the observation of attributes or measurements. An item that is supposed to be a certain size can be measured directly and the data regarding its dimensional size can be collected. All items accepted will be within the acceptable allowed tolerance on the item.

Items may also be inspected by attribute. In this technique the item to be inspected is made to fit or not fit into a specially designed gauge or special measuring device. If the part fits into the "Go" gauge and does not fit into the "No-Go" gauge, then the part is accepted. If the part does not fit into the "Go" gauge or fits into the "No-Go" gauge, the part is considered to be bad. All attribute inspections have a yes or no outcome.

Attribute sampling has several advantages over measurement methods. In attribute sampling the inspection is fast and relatively inexpensive, and there is little room for errors. Measurements take a certain amount of skill and concentration. As such, measurements are prone to human errors stemming from fatigue and boredom.

For example, suppose a motor shaft has a design tolerance of 1 ½ inches and an allowable tolerance of plus or minus 0.015 inches for its diameter. This means that an acceptable part will have to be between 1.515 and 1.485 inches. To test this attribute, a gauge is constructed with a hole that has a diameter of exactly 1.515 inches. This will become the "Go" gauge. Parts that have a diameter less than 1.515 inches will fir into this gauge, and those that are larger than 1.515 inches will not fit. Another gauge is also constructed with a hole of 1.485 inches diameter. Parts that fit into this gauge will be unacceptable, since their diameter is less than specified minimum diameter of 1.485 inches. This gauge becomes the "No-Go" gauge. The inspection of shafts is quick, easy, and nearly foolproof. A part is first applied to the "Go" gauge. If it passes through the hole of this gauge, it is immediately put into the "No-Go" gauge. If it fails to fit this gauge, it is considered acceptable.

Sampling Inspection and Other Quality Control Techniques

Unless there are unusual requirements for extreme quality, as when death or severe injuries can result from a defective part, most customers will accept a certain amount of defects. The reason for this is stated in the law of diminishing returns. As the desire to locate every defect is satisfied, it becomes more and more costly to find them. One hundred percent inspections are expensive and require much time and effort. In 100 percent inspections there is also the problem of the inspection itself causing damage to some of the parts. This entire concept is based on the fact that the customer is willing to accept a small number of defective parts rather than pay the high cost of trying to locate each and every defect.

This policy of allowing a few unacceptable parts must be considered carefully. The ultimate use of the parts must be considered. In particular, it is important that the part that is defective not create life threatening situations. There can be settlements against companies that attempted to do so.

For this reason, statistical sampling was developed. Sampling inspection plans have been worked out and are available to quality managers to determine the parameters desired and to set up an inspection plan that will fit the type of work that they are doing.

In a sampling inspection, the sample size to be taken and inspected from a given lot size is determined. A sample size of fifteen parts may be taken from a lot of parts. Again, according to pre-calculated procedures, the fifteen-piece sample can contain no more than three unacceptable parts. If less than three parts in the sample are unacceptable, the lot passes, and if more than three parts are unacceptable, then the lot is rejected.

The rationale behind this technique is that if the acceptable quality level (AQL) was 3 percent and a sample of fifteen parts was taken from a lot of a thousand parts, there would be a very small chance that some of the bad parts would show up in the sample. If more than three were to show up in the sample, it could be said that the whole lot had more bad parts than 3 percent allowed by the AQL.

Acceptable Quality Level (AQL)

Because discovering all of the defective parts can be a very costly and time consuming process, most customers and suppliers agree that a certain level of defects is to be allowed in the normal process. As long as this acceptable quality level, or AQL, is maintained, the lot of parts is acceptable to customer. In the previous example, a lot of parts that had less than 3 percent bad parts in it was accepted.

Buyer's and Seller's Risks

When we perform sampling inspections, there is a risk that the sample will give misleading information. There are four possible outcomes to this inspection process. The possibilities are as follows:

I.   The lot is good and the sample inspection says that it is good. This is what we want.

II. The lot is good and the sample inspection says that it is not good. This is what we don't want.

III. The lot is bad and the sample inspection says that it is good. This is what we don't want.

IV. The lot is bad and the sample inspection says that it is bad. *This is what we want.*

If the sampling inspection accepts a lot that is good or rejects a lot that is bad, then the inspection process is working. If the sampling process accepts a lot of parts that is really bad, this means that a lot that is unacceptable is shipped as a good lot to the customer. This is called "buyer's risk". If the sampling process rejects a lot that is really good; this means that a lot of parts that is acceptable is rejected. This is called "seller's risk".

Flowcharts and Diagrams

Flowcharts can be helpful in understanding the cause and effect relationships between the process of performing work and the results that are inspected through measurement or attribute inspection. A flowchart is simply an organized way to look at the steps that have to be carried out to perform some goal. There are many techniques and styles of flowcharting. Some of these flowcharts are described below.

Cause and Effect Diagrams: The cause and effect the cause and effect diagram (aka the fishbone diagram) was developed by Kaoru Ishikawa. This is a form of diagramming the cause and effect of problems that are encountered. The following figure is an example of a generic cause-and-effect diagram.

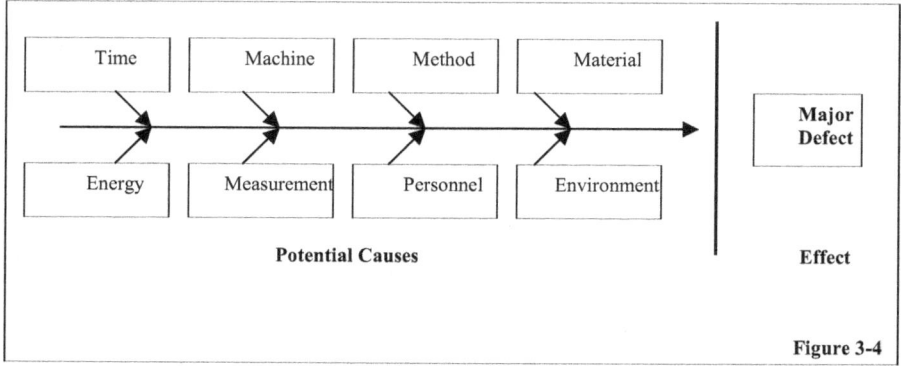

Potential Causes

Effect

Figure 3-4

Pareto Charts: Vilfredo Pareto is given credit for developing the concept of 80-20 rule. He was an economist who found that typically 80 percent of the wealth of a region was concentrated in 20 percent of the population. This concept describes a number of phenomena that occur in the real world. In terms of quality, it can be said that 80 percent of the cost of defects are caused by 20 percent of the problems. In other words, if there were one hundred possible things that could be considered to be defects in a process, 20 percent, or twenty of the problems, will account for 80 percent of the cost.

By identifying these twenty items it is possible to expend the energy of the organization where it will do the most good. In quality control as well as many other areas of project management, it is important that the always-limited effort available in the organization be concentrated on the problems where the most benefits will result.

The Pareto chart is a simple way of determining the places where this effort might be concentrated. The problems in a process are arranged in the order of importance and are generally arranged by ranking according to the most important factors, such as cost, time delay, or some other parameters.

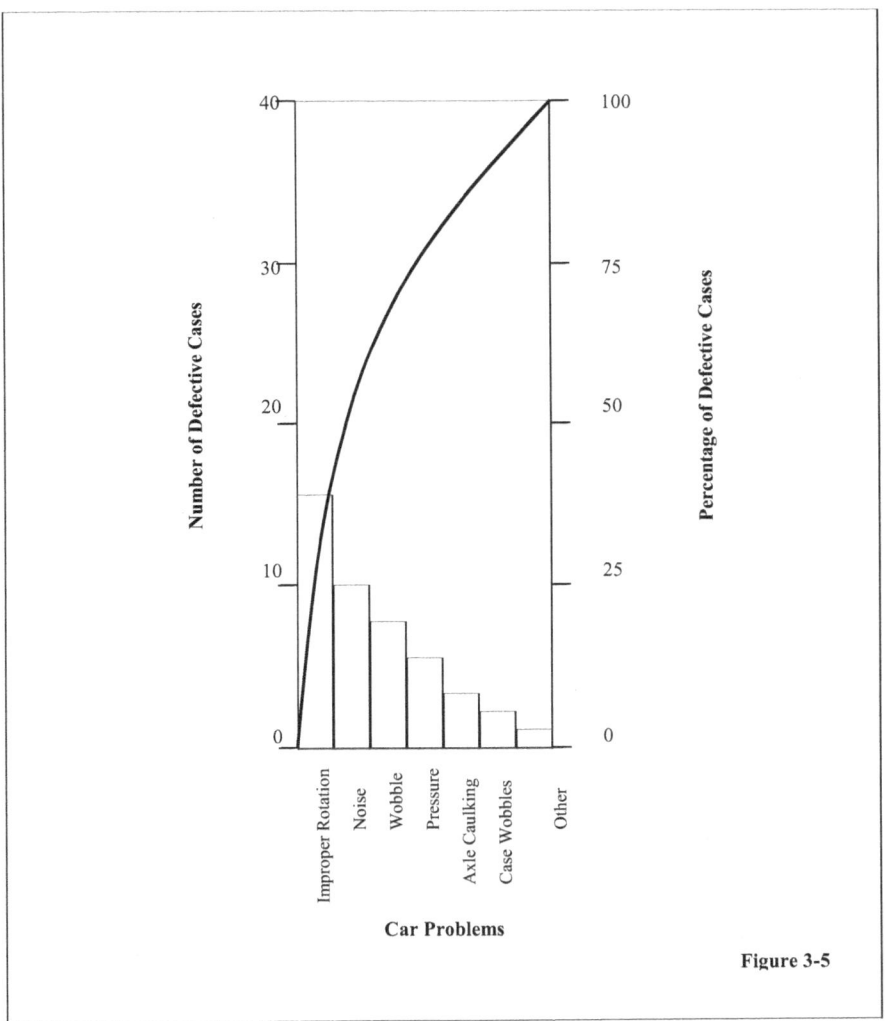

Figure 3-5

Control Charts: Control charts are a graphic display of the results, over time, of a process. They are used to determine if the process is "in control" (e.g., are differences in the results created by random variations, or are unusual events occurring whose causes must be identified and corrected?). When a process is in control, the process should not be adjusted. The process may be changed to provide improvements, but it should not be adjusted when it is in control.

Control charts may be used to monitor ant type of output variable. Although used most frequently to track repetitive activities, such as manufactured lots, control charts can also be used to monitor cost and schedule variances, volume and frequency of scope changes, errors in project documents, or other management results to help determine if the *project management process* is in control. The following Figure is a control chart of project schedule performance.

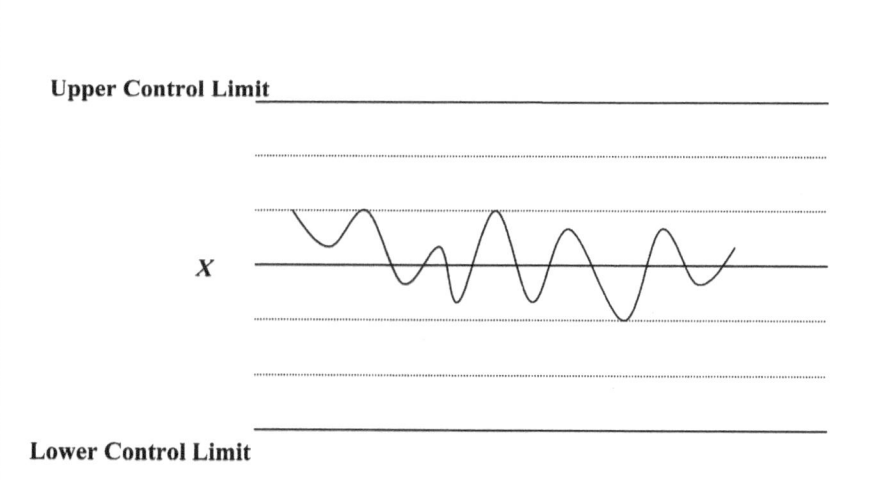

Upper Control Limit

X

Lower Control Limit

The x axis of all control charts consists of sample numbers (usually the time of the sample). Control charts have three common lines:

    I.   A center line, designated with an "*X*", which provides the average (x) of the process data.

    II.   An upper line designating the upper control limit (UCL), drawn at a calculated distance above the center line, showing the upper range of data.

    III.   The lower line designating the lower control limit (LCL), which shows the lower range of data.

Points outside of the UCL and LCL are indicative that the process is out of control and/or unstable.

Checklists: Checklists are a sample tool that is used to keep from overlooking items of importance. A checklist is really just an instruction sheet for an inspector to use. The items in the checklist should be significant items and must correspond to the project specifications for quality control and assurance. If a checklist is seen as a superfluous document, it will not be used.

Kaizen: Kaizen is one of the many quality techniques that come to us from the work of the Japanese. The Japanese word for continuous improvement is called Kaizen. Using this method, the managers as well as workers and everyone else are continuously on the lookout for opportunities to improve quality. Thus the quality of a process improves in small increments on a continuous basis.

Benchmarking: Benchmarking is the process of comparing the performance of your current process to that of another process that is similar. If an old machine can manufacture two hundred parts an hour, and a new machine is compared to the old machine, the benchmark for the existing process on the old machine is two hundred parts per hour.

4

PROJECT SCOPE MANAGEMENT

Project Initiation
Scope Planning
Scope Change Control

Project Scope Management

Without a doubt, the most common reason that projects fail is because of poor scope definition. By that I mean that the expectations of the stakeholders, and especially the client or sponsor, are different than the expectations of the project team. This is most difficult problem to overcome, bit it is critical to the success of the project that it is overcome. There are many reasons for this, and understanding them will help us understand how to avoid them.

The relationship between the project team and the customer has to reverse itself at the time of scope definition. Up to this point the customer's main contact has been someone from a sales organization. During this part of the project the salesperson has tried to convince the customer that this project is a good project to do. Sometimes the salesperson has been overly enthusiastic about the project and intentionally or unintentionally led the customer to believe that everything the customer could imagine is actually going to be produced by the project. This is rarely the case.

When the project team is formed and members begin to hold meetings with the customer to develop the scope of the project the customer has the notion that the project is already defined. As a result the customer views the whole process of scope definition as a waste of time. In fact the customer may actually resist the scope definition process because of fear of committing to defining the project.

It becomes very difficult for the project team to convince the customer that both the project team and the customer have the same goals for the project. That is, the goal of the project is to give the customer something that is actually useful and something that does what the customer wanted in the first place. There is no point in having an adversarial relationship between the customer and the project team. Both parties want the project to succeed, and both want the project to be useful and serve the purpose for which it was intended.

The project team needs to understand the customer as well. Members of the team should not be frustrated if the customer seems to know less than they do. After all, the reason that the project team is doing the project is because they are expert at accomplishing the project. The customer representatives, in spite of what they might say or think, are not expert in doing the project. That is why the project team was formed in the first place.

Sometimes extraordinary means must be used to develop the scope of work in the customer's area for a period of time and become trained in the work that the project is supposed to enhance. This is a good technique when the customer is not willing or able to cooperate in devoting the necessary time and manpower to working with the project team. The project team member simply becomes a surrogate customer and learns enough about the customer's operation to speak for the customer.

Of course, it is much more desirable to have the customer play this role. The customer should be included in the project team, as should all of the project stakeholders. The greater the involvement and the greater the level of communications that you have with all of the stakeholders, the sounder project will be. This starts with defining the scope of the project.

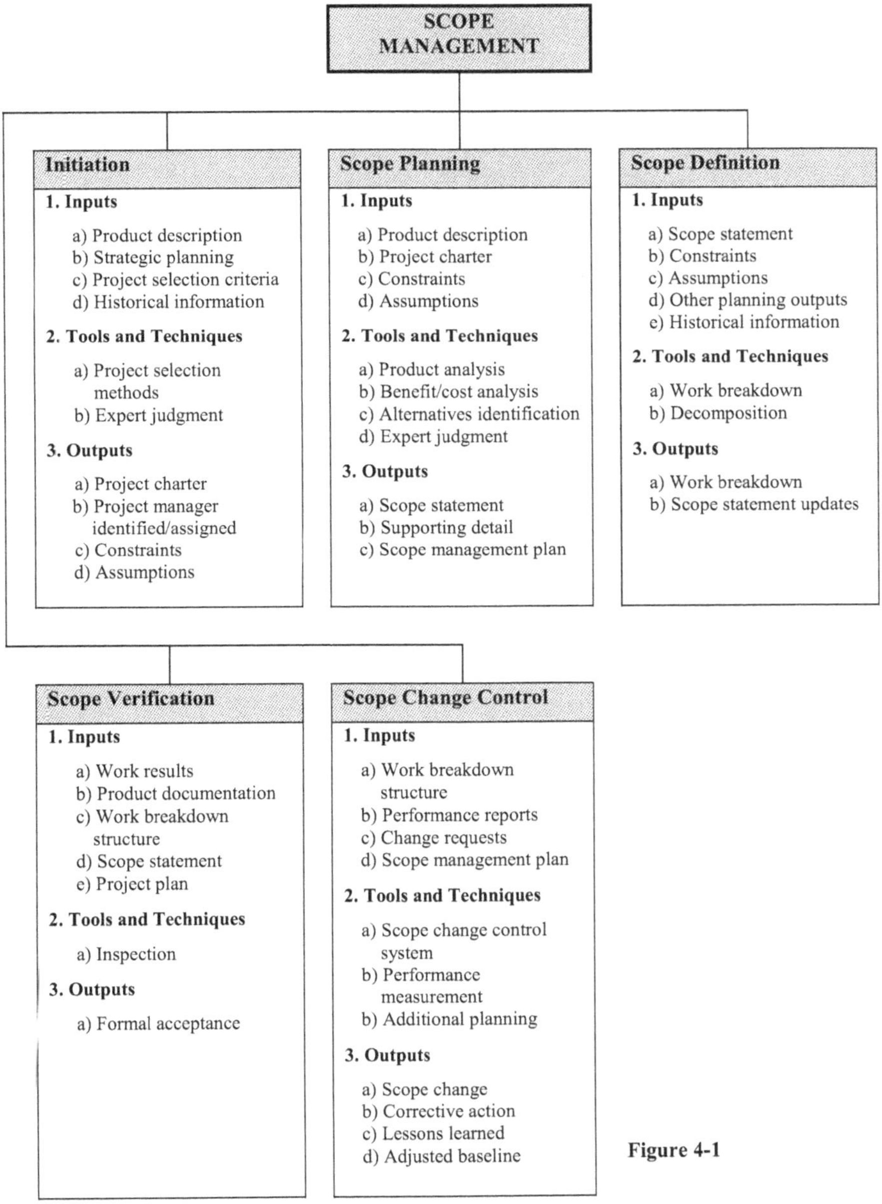
SCOPE MANAGEMENT
Initiation
1. Inputs
a) Product description
b) Strategic planning
c) Project selection criteria
d) Historical information
2. Tools and Techniques
a) Project selection methods
b) Expert judgment
3. Outputs
a) Project charter
b) Project manager identified/assigned
c) Constraints
d) Assumptions
Scope Planning
1. Inputs
a) Product description
b) Project charter
c) Constraints
d) Assumptions
2. Tools and Techniques
a) Product analysis
b) Benefit/cost analysis
c) Alternatives identification
d) Expert judgment
3. Outputs
a) Scope statement
b) Supporting detail
c) Scope management plan
Scope Definition
1. Inputs
a) Scope statement
b) Constraints
c) Assumptions
d) Other planning outputs
e) Historical information
2. Tools and Techniques
a) Work breakdown
b) Decomposition
3. Outputs
a) Work breakdown
b) Scope statement updates
Scope Verification
1. Inputs
a) Work results
b) Product documentation
c) Work breakdown structure
d) Scope statement
e) Project plan
2. Tools and Techniques
a) Inspection
3. Outputs
a) Formal acceptance
Scope Change Control
1. Inputs
a) Work breakdown structure
b) Performance reports
c) Change requests
d) Scope management plan
2. Tools and Techniques
a) Scope change control system
b) Performance measurement
b) Additional planning
3. Outputs
a) Scope change
b) Corrective action
c) Lessons learned
d) Adjusted baseline

Figure 4-1

Project Initiation

Initiation is the process of formally authorizing a new project to start or that an existing project should continue into its next phase. This formal initiation links the project to the ongoing work of the performing organization. In some organizations, a project is not formally initiated until after completion of a needs assessment, a feasibility study, a preliminary plan, or some other equivalent form of analysis that was itself separately initiated. Some types of projects, especially internal service projects and new product development projects are initiated informally, and some limited amount of work is done to secure the approvals needed for formal initiation. Projects are typically authorized as a result of one or more of the following:

- A market demand (e.g., car company authorizes a project to build more fuel efficient cars in response to gasoline shortages).

- A business need (e.g., a training company authorizes a project to create a new course to increase its revenue).

- A customer request (e.g., am electric utility authorizes a project to build a new substation to serve a new industrial park).

- A legal requirement (e.g., a paint manufacturer authorizes a project to establish guidelines for the handling of toxic materials).

- A social need (e.g., a nongovernmental organization in a developing country authorizes a project to provide potable water systems, latrines, and sanitation education to low-income communities suffering from high rates of cholera).

These stimuli may also be called problems, business requirements, or opportunities. The central theme of all these terms is that management generally must make a decision about how to respond.

Project Charter: A project starts with the creation of the project charter, a formal document that brings the project into existence. The essential components of the project charter are simple. It formally authorizes the project to begin and names the project manager and the management team. This is usually done by creating some sort of account that will allow costs to be accumulated for this project. It will also contain a brief business case for the project showing the justification for the project.

One interesting thing about the project charter is that it must be written by the project manager but it must be distributed under the signature of the person that is authorized to create the project and funding for the project. It would make no sense to have project managers creating and authorizing their own projects. However, it is important that the project manager actually write the project charter. This is because it is the first opportunity for the project manager to define the project as he or she sees it.

Constraints and Assumptions: In addition to the project charter, any constraints that limit the project team's choices in any of the project activities must be noted. Predetermined project schedules, project completion dates, and project budgets need to be reckoned with early in the project.

Assumptions must be made for the purpose of planning the project. These are considerations for the availability of resources, vendors, start dates, contract signing, and so on. Assumptions are necessary for any project. To successfully plan a project many assumptions have to be made or the project will never get started.

Stakeholders: Stakeholders are generally all of the people that have something to gain or lose in the project both directly or indirectly. We are generally concerned only with the key stakeholders of a project. We must be careful that we consider all of the stakeholders in a project, albeit some to a lesser extent than others.

The first problem is to identify the key stakeholders. How can we best accomplish this task? For some reason there is reluctance on the part of project managers to contact all of the key stakeholders in the project, let alone the ones that are not so critical. This may result in a poor definition of what the project is all about. With a poor definition of the project, there is no hope of ever being able to construct a project plan and determine the cost, schedule, and scope objectives that project managers hold so dear to their hearts.

One of the techniques that can be used is to have seven to ten members of your project team get together and use one of the group dynamics techniques to come up with the names of all the stakeholders for the project. One technique that is gaining in popularity these days is called "The Crawford Slip".

Each person in the team is given ten pieces of paper. The facilitator asks the question, "Who is the most important stakeholder in this project?" The participants answer each question with the best answer they can think of. This is done in silence, and the answers are not discussed at this time. The facilitator waits one minute and asks the same question again. Each time the question is asked, the participants must answer the question. An answer cannot be used more than once for each participant.

After the question has been asked ten times, the group should have generated seventy to ninety responses. If the team was picked carefully, so that there is diversity among the participants, there is a good chance that a high percentage of the stakeholders have been identified.

At this point the list of stakeholders can be compiled and distributed to the participants for additions and corrections. With this technique we have gone long way toward identifying the stakeholders in the project.

Cost and its Relationship to Price: One of the things that seem to be confusing is the relationship between cost and price. Thus, the first thing we should do is to make certain that we are all using the same meanings for these two words.

Price is the amount of money (or something else) that a customer or stakeholder is willing to give you in order to receive something from you. Generally, in terms of project management, the thing that is being done for the stakeholder is the project and the things that are being delivered are the deliverables of the project. These things can be either goods or services. Money is usually the thing that is given in exchange for doing the project.

Cost, on the other hand, is the amount of resources (money, people, materials, equipment, etc.) that are consumed in order to produce the delivered goods or services that the project has as its result.

What is the relationship between cost and price? Are we satisfied if we are able to make a reasonable profit on what we do for stakeholders? Are we satisfied if the cost of doing a project is less than the selling price by some acceptable percentage?

Let us explore this a bit further. Suppose we say yes, we would be satisfied if our total project cost was 85 percent of the selling price. We must first ask where the selling price came from. Did our sales and marketing people try to get the highest price they could or were they satisfied by being able to get the acceptable 15 percent markup from the customer?

Eliyahu Goldratt said in his book "It's not lick" that the price of something should be determined by the perceived value to the buyer. What this means is that the selling price of anything we do should be determined by what the customers and the stakeholders are willing to pay. Having determined what the stakeholders are willing to pay, we then need to determine whether it is profitable enough for us to do the work. To determine this we must determine cost.

Overbid or Underbid: As discussed above, it is important to price things according to the perceived value to the customer. In other words, if a project has a high value to stakeholders or customers, they should pay a price that is high as well.

Now, suppose we are in a bidding situation. Our organization is in the kind of business where the stakeholders publish requirements and companies like ours submit a firm fixed price to do the work specified. Many construction projects work this way, but many other types of projects are done this way as well. These situations are usually done in a competitive way, and other companies are bidding for the same project.

The question is: Is it better for companies to underbid or overbid projects like this? Most people would say, "It is better to overbid the project, because if I underbid I may win the project but lose money trying to complete it. Let us explore this response a bit further. A company that underbids a project and wins the bid finds that its cost estimate for doing the work is too low, and as a result, it did not charge the stakeholders enough to make a profit. In fact, it may actually lose money on this project.

This gives the company immediate feedback. The company knows soon after starting the work that there will not be enough money coming from the customer to pay all the costs and expense associated with the project. At this point, lots of unhappy things take place.

The company may go to the customer or stakeholders and ask for additional funds. The company may have to grin and bear it and lose money or at least not make as much profit as it would like to. The company may try to reduce the requirements to save costs, with or without the customer's approval. Panic may follow, leading to an unhappy situation all around.

But every cloud has a silver lining. The company in this situation at least knows where it stands, and one way or another, the next time it bids on a job it will increase price. Companies in this situation either learn from this experience or soon find another line of work.

Remember the other situation we had talked about. The company overbids the work. In this situation, only two things can happen. The company bids too high and does not get the job, or the company bids high and gets the job anyway. In the first situation, the company loses the bid and does not get to work on the project. This may or may not have a positive effect on future business. If the company is convinced that the bid it submitted was just too high, it might look into its cost-estimating process and at some of the costs associated with the way it does things.

Many times companies just don't do this. They become convinced that for some other reason the competition got the job and they did not. You will hear about how so-and-so's brother-in-law was a friend of the purchasing agent or so-and-so's wife is in a bridge club with the company's owner, and so on. Companies are reluctant to admit that they may be doing something wrong, and they wait for the next opportunity to come along.

Now let us consider the situation where the company overbids the project and is awarded the contract anyway. This could actually be the worst thing for the company. In the underbid situation we discussed that there was some feedback to the company that something was wrong, and there was some force present to indicate that it should do business differently in the future.

When a company overbids a project and is awarded the contract, what budget will the company assign to the project manager of this project? It will probability take the bid price, reduce it by some acceptable level of profit, and ask the project manager to complete the project with those funds.

This sounds right except that in this situation the company overbid the project. As a result, the company is going to overbudget the project. The reason is that it doesn't really know that it overbid the project in the first place.

The project manager measures the progress and the performance of his or her project according to the allocated budget. As long as the project is completed on time, under budget and the requirements are all satisfied, no one is likely to complain about the project performance.

As time goes by, more jobs like this are bid and won, and the company continues on with an acceptable profit. Its projects get done, and everyone is happy. Ignorance is bliss.

Sooner or later a competitor is going to figure out that there is extra profit to be made in this type of business. They discover this by doing a better cost analysis than our company and bid the same jobs but at a lower price.

At first, there is no reaction. Lost work is considered just the normal business cycle. As time goes by and there is less and less business, the company may eventually come to its sense and realize that its costs are too high, and take some corrective action.

This is very hard for companies to do. They are in the situation where for years they have done things the way they have and been successful. Now they are losing business, and they have a lot of trouble figuring out why.

If they had good cost estimates, they still might have been able to overbid the projects, but the budget for the projects would have been larger.

What must happen next is that the companies must take those excessive profits and invest them in their own operations, so that they modernize before being forced to by their competition.

We can see that the worst thing that could happen to companies is that they overestimate cost. From that, they overbid work and overbudget projects. Then they learn inefficient ways to do things, and from all of that, they possibly go out of business.

Scope Planning

Scope Baseline: The first thing that happens in a project is usually characterized by the feeling of wild and unbridled enthusiasm. This results in a great many things being included as "needs" of the project. In many respects this is a good thing. If there are many good things that can result from the project, it is probably a good project to do. The problem is that many of these things are not necessary or are impractical. Many of the "results" may not be what the stakeholders need or really want.

The next step, then is to have the project team and the stakeholders come together and separate out the "needs" that everyone agrees are not going to be practical or necessary for the project to be useful. When we reduce the number of needs of the project by deleting the ones that everyone agrees are not part of the project, the result is the "requirements" of the project.

We are not finished at this point. We have only reduced the project by the items that everyone agrees to eliminate. We must further reduce this list of requirements by removing those that may not be good for the project. These items are not so obvious and will not have the agreement of all the stakeholders. There will have to be some investigation and some justification applied to make these items acceptable or not acceptable to the project. When this analysis is completed, the result is the project's scope baseline. This is the first baseline that we develop, and it is necessary to have the scope baseline before the remaining two baselines, cost and schedule, can be completed.

When moving from requirements to scope baseline, the items that are eliminated from the project must be documented as exclusions to the project. It is important to do this, since at one time these items were thought to be good for the project by at least some of the stakeholders. If their exclusion is not properly documented, they will return again and again as new requirements to be considered.

For all of these items that will or will not be included in the project there are a number of factors that must be considered, such as cost, expense, time to develop, service, and maintenance. It is critically important that all of the stakeholders be involved with the parts of the project that they have a stake in. To accomplish this there must be a good cooperative relationship between the stakeholders and the project team. Very detailed descriptions of the intentions of the project must be obtained.

All items making it to the scope baseline must be fully documented and clearly defined. There must be tangible project results that are measurable. These should be documented along with the acceptable criteria as part of the scope definition. When this is not done, scope cannot be controlled. Project scope tends to creep ever upward with requests from the stakeholders that start out, "There is this one little change that we need to make to the project" or, "This item should have been included in the original scope of the project".

When we completed all of this, we will have developed a set of deliverables that the stakeholders and the project team can agree upon. These deliverables must be formally agreed to by all, and there should be a *formal* sign off. All of the participants in the project must agree that the deliverables list is a conclusive, exhaustive list of things that the project is going to produce. There should be no doubt that the deliverables list that has been agreed to is final unless a formal change is approved. Participants should also realize that any approved changes to the project after this point are going to result in increase in cost and possibly a change in the project schedule.

To make all this possible, each of the project deliverables must be clear and concise. Each deliverable must be tangible, measurable criteria that determine that it has been completed and accepted by the stakeholder. Every effort must be made to avoid describing deliverables in a way that can be misunderstood.

Work Breakdown: A WBS is a deliverable-oriented grouping of project components that organizes and defines the total scope of the project; work not in the WBS is outside the scope of the project. The WBS is often used to develop or confirm a common understanding of project scope. Each descending level represents an increasingly detailed description of the project deliverables. The most common approach to developing a WBS is called "Decomposition". Decomposition involves subdividing the major project deliverables or subdeliverables into smaller, more manageable components until the deliverables are defined in sufficient detail to support development of project activities (planning, execution, controlling, and closing). Decomposition involves the following major steps:

1) Identify the major deliverables of the project, including project management. The major deliverables should always be defined in terms of how the project will actually be organized. For example, the phases of the project life cycle may be used as the first level of decomposition with the project deliverables repeated at the second level, as illustrated in Figure 4-2. Another example is as illustrated in Figure 4-3 that the organizing principle within each branch of the WBS may vary.

2) Decide if adequate cost and duration estimates can be developed at this level of detail for each deliverable. The meaning of *adequate* may change over the course of the project—decomposition of a deliverable, proceed to Step 4 if there is adequate detail, to Step 3 if

there is not—this means that different deliverables may have differing levels of decomposition.

3) Identify constituent components of the deliverable. Constituent components should be described in terms of tangible, verifiable results to facilitate performance measurements. As with the major components, the constituent components should be defined in terms of how the work of the project will actually be organized and the work of the project accomplished. Tangible, verifiable results can include services as well as products (e.g., status reporting could be described as weekly status reports; for a manufactured item, constituent components might include several individual components plus final assembly). Repeat Step 2 on each constituent component.

4) Verify the correctness of the decomposition:

o Are the lower-level items both necessary and sufficient for completion of the decomposed item? If not, the constituent components must be modified (added to, deleted from, or redefined).

o Is each item clearly and completely defined? If not, the descriptions must be revised or expanded.

o Can each item be appropriately scheduled? Budgeted? Assigned to a specific organizational unit (e.g., department, team, or person) who will accept responsibility for satisfactory completion of the item? If not, revisions are needed to provide adequate management control.

As mentioned before, a WBS is normally presented in chart form, as illustrated in Figures 4-2 and 4-3; however, the WBS should not be confused with the method of presentation-drawing and unstructured activity list in chart form does not make it a WBS.

Each item in the WBS is generally assigned a unique identifier; these identifiers can provide a structure for a hierarchical summation of costs and resources. The items at the lowest level of the WBS may be referred to as *work packages*, especially in organizations that follow earned value management practices. These work packages may in turn be further decomposed in a subproject work breakdown structure. Generally, this type of approach is used when the project manager is assigning a scope of work to another organization, and this other organization must plan and manager the scope of work at a more detailed level than the project manager in the main project. These work packages may be further decomposed in the main project schedule.

Work component descriptions are often collected in a WBS dictionary. A WBS dictionary will typically include work package descriptions, as well as other planning information such as schedule dates, cost budgets, and staff assignments.

The WBS should not be confused with other types of "breakdown" structures used to present project information. Other structures commonly used in some application areas include:

o   Contractual WBS (CWBS), which is used to define the level of reporting that the seller will provide the buyer. The CWBS generally includes less detail than the WBS used by the seller to manage the seller's work.

o   Organizational breakdown structure (OSB), which is used to show which work components have been assigned to which organizational units.

o   Resource breakdown structure (RBS), which is a variation of the OBS and is typically used when work components are assigned to individuals.

o   Bill of materials (BOM), which presents a hierarchical view of the physical assemblies, subassemblies, and components needed to fabricate a manufactured product.

o   Project breakdown structure (PBS), which is fundamentally the same as a properly done WBS. The term PBS is widely used in application areas where the term WBS is incorrectly used to refer to a BOM

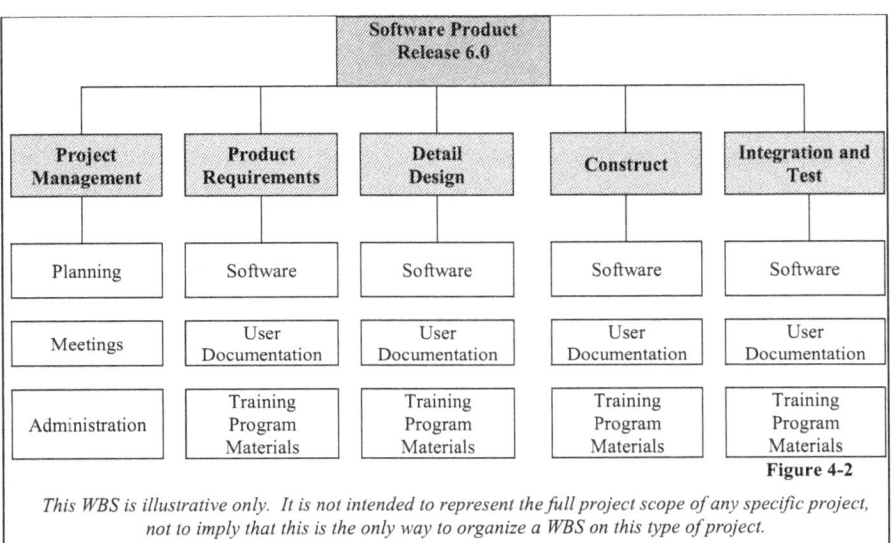

Figure 4-2

This WBS is illustrative only. It is not intended to represent the full project scope of any specific project, not to imply that this is the only way to organize a WBS on this type of project.

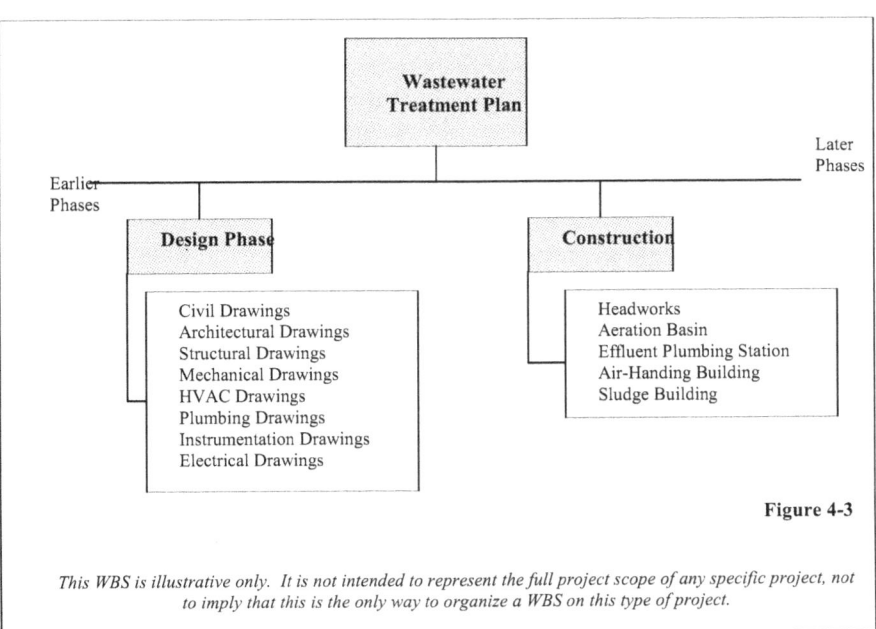

Figure 4-3

This WBS is illustrative only. It is not intended to represent the full project scope of any specific project, not to imply that this is the only way to organize a WBS on this type of project.

Scope Change Management

A change control process must be put in place to control the project once the scope baseline has been set. The change control process is a formal process that controls the project scope baseline. The change management process must be in place early in the project, certainly no later than the completion of the scope baseline.

The point of change management process is to establish recognition scope. Changes in scope and funding do not necessarily mean increase in project scope and funding. Many times there can be agreed upon changes that reduce the project scope, or it may increase it.

In the change management process, certain essentials must be included regardless of whether the project changes are funded internally or externally to the project. The proposed change must first be evaluated as to how much time and effort it will take to evaluate the implementation of the change. Stakeholders who ask that new things be incorporated into the project can bog down a project team. The investigation of these changes can cost much in time and effort. Thus, the first thing that needs to take place in the change management process is that the stakeholders must authorize funding to investigate the change. Once the funding is approved, the project team can bring in additional resources to complete the investigation. The investigation must include the effect that the change will have on all aspects of the project. Once the effect on cost, schedule, and scope of the project is determined, a justification for the change can take place. If the justification is adequate and the stakeholders wish to authorize the funds for the change, the change can move into the project plan.

The change management process is actually a small project plan. All of the steps that must be taken in planning a project must be taken for project changes as well. When all of this has been done, the project baselines of cost, schedule, and scope are changed accordingly, and the new project plan is implemented.

Project Justifications: There are many reasons for doing projects, and some are more tangible than others. Projects may be justified by having to respond to a government order, such as a redesign of an unsafe automobile or changing a process that is found to be polluting air or water. Other projects may be justified by the opportunity to create new business or enter a new field.

Of course, one of the strongest and most compelling project justifications is the benefit occurring to the organization that provides the project team. The most efficient way to measure this is by comparing the monetary benefits and the monetary cost of the project. For this reason many justification methods have been developed over the years. It is important to use the appropriate method for project justification. The selection of a justification technique has its own costs and benefits. Some methods produce results that consider some of these factors. The more aspects of the project that are considered, the higher will be the cost of the justification.

All analysis techniques are form of cash flow analysis. Cash flow analysis is simply measuring the cash flowing into and out of an organization over time. Projects that have more cash flowing into the organization than cash flowing out are good projects. Projects that have more cash flowing into the organization faster are better projects. In most projects it is necessary to make an investment in the project (cash outflow) before the benefits can begin (cash inflow).

Present Value of Money: Before we consider the more sophisticated methods of justification, we need to look at the present value of money and the net present value of money.

Suppose I borrow $100 from you today and pay you back $100 tomorrow. This is a reasonable transaction between friends. But suppose I borrow $100 from you today and don't pay it back to you for two years. Is this still a fair arrangement? You should say no! I have had the use of your money for two years and have paid you nothing for the use of your money. If I had not borrowed the money from you, you could have invested the money in something and you would have had something more than $100 you started with. In fact, you could have invested in something as safe as Mutual Funds and made perhaps $15 in interest payments.

This is the idea behind using the present value of money. The money that I receive in the future is worth less than the money I receive now. This is not to say that money I receive in the future is worthless, it is just worth less than money I get today. The further into the future I get money, the less valuable it is to me today. In the given example above, I should have given you $115 for borrowing $100 from you for two years.

The calculation that I use to figure out what $100 will be worth two years from now is the compound interest formula.

If you put your $100 in a bank savings account at 7 percent interest for one year, you would receive $107.

$$FV = PV + (PV * I)$$

Where

PV	=	present value of money
FV	=	future value of the same money
I	=	interest rate

Thus, $107 = 100 + (100 * .07)$

And, if you leave the money in the bank at the same interest rate, you would get more the next year:

$FV = 107 + (107 * .07)$

$$FV = 107 + 7.49$$
$$FV = 114.49$$

With a little manipulation, the series of calculations can be generalized into the compound interest formula:

$$FV = PV (1 + I)n$$

The new term in this formula is "n", the number of time periods that the interest is applied.

Your $100 invested at 7 percent for two years look like this:

$$FV = 100 (1 = .07)2$$
$$FV = 100 (1.07)2$$
$$FV = 100 (1.1449)$$
$$FV = 114.49$$

Now that we have reviewed compound interest calculations, it is time to look at calculating the present value of money that we get in the future. This is really just the compound interest calculation solved for the present value instead of the future value.

Start with the compound interest formula as described above. Convert the formula to solve for the present value:

$$PV = FV / (1 + I)n$$

Let us say that we can do something that will result in a return of $100 two years from now, and we would like to know what the equivalent present value of the money is. Remember, money that we receive in the future is worth less than the money we receive now. Here we are trying to determine the present value of the $100 we will receive in two years.

$$PV = FV / (1 + I)n$$
$$PV = 100 / 1.072$$
$$PV = 100 / 1.1449$$
$$PV = 87.34$$

You can check this number by calculating the compound interest future value of $87.34 invested at 7 percent for two years. The result should be $100.

Let us bring this into context of a project. Projects usually start out with someone investing an amount of money at the beginning of the project and later receiving benefits from the project. By using the present value calculations we can more accurately determine the true value of the project. Projects that have very high returns early in the project's useful life are considered better projects than those projects that have the same returns that came later in the project.

The term "net present value" is the sum of all the cash flows of a project adjusted to present values. For example, suppose we have two projects that have the same initial cost of $100,000. The two projects have the same net cash flows as well, but the time that the money comes to us is different. The interest rate for borrowing money is 7 percent. Figures 4-4 and 4-5 illustrate the present value cash flow.

Notice that here the two projects have the same total return over the ten year life of the projects, but Project A gets more of the returns sooner, making the net present value of the money higher. Remember, the present value of the money is the value today of money that will be received in the future.

In this justification analysis, we considered much more than in previous methods. Here we recognized all of the costs and revenues that occur over the useful life of the project. If this were a project to buy a machine, for example, we would look at the cash flows over the expected life of the machine. This allows us to consider the effect of changing sales forecasts and changing maintenance costs, and then we can adjust for the time value of the money that is involved in the project. This method gives us a good idea of which projects we should select.

But there is still one difficulty with this method. There is a problem distinguishing small projects that have small investments and relatively small returns when compared to large projects. This method of justification tells us only the net present value of the project. It does not tell us whether we would be better off selecting a number of small projects or only a few large ones. What we need is a method of justification that gives us a single value that will be highest for the most favorable project, regardless of its size. Such a method would allow us to rank all of potential projects by this value and use the ranking order to pick the projects that are the most lucrative.

Project A				7% Interest	
Year	Outflow	Inflow		PV	NPV
0	-100,000	0			-100,000
1		60,000		56,075	-43,925
2		50,000		43,672	-253
3		40,000		32,652	32,399
4		30,000		22,887	55,286
5		20,000		14,260	69,546
6		20,000		13,327	82,873
7		20,000		12,455	95,328
8		20,000		11,640	106,986
9		20,000		10,876	117,847
10		20,000		10,167	128,014
Total:	**-100,000**	**300,000**		**228,014**	

Figure 4-4

Project B				7% Interest	
Year	Outflow	Inflow		PV	NPV
0	-100,000	0			-100,000
1		30,000		28,037	-71,963
2		30,000		26,203	-45,760
3		30,000		24,489	-21,271
4		30,000		22,887	1,616
5		30,000		21,390	23,006
6		30,000		19,990	42,996
7		30,000		18,682	61,678
8		30,000		17,460	79,138
9		30,000		16,318	95,456
10		30,000		15,250	110,706
Total:	**-100,000**	**300,000**		**210,706**	

Figure 4-5

5

TIME MANAGEMENT

Activity Definition
Activity Sequencing
Schedule Development and Control
Critical Path Method (CPM)
Program Evaluation and Review Technique (PERT)
Monte Carlo Simulation

Time Management

The *Guide to the PMBOK* describes project time management as the process used to ensure the timely completion of the project. The guide goes on to say that there are five major processes that are required to do proper project time management:

- Activity definition—Defining the specific activities that are necessary to complete the project and produce all of the project deliverables.

- Activity sequencing—Identifying the sequence in which the activities must be done. This is the same as identifying the interdependencies of the activities and inputs external to the project.

- Activity duration estimating—Estimating the duration of time that is necessary for each activity.

- Schedule development—Analyzing all of the data available to determine the project schedule that will work for the project.

- Schedule control—Controlling changes that occur in the project that affect the project schedule.

Activity Definition

The main tool required for the definition of the activity as well as the determination of the duration and sequence of activities is the work breakdown structure (WBS). As discussed before, work breakdown structure is used to methodically break down the project into manageable subprojects.

The end result of this breakdown is the creation of the lowest level of breakdown. This lowest level of breakdown comprises the individual pieces of work that must be done to complete the project. The WBS represents the lowest level of control that the project manager is required to manage. This is the work package level. From the viewpoint of the subproject manager, this level of control may reach down to the work package, be broken down further to the activity level, or be broken still further to the individual task level.

The WBS represents all of the work that the project team must do to complete the project. Before scheduling work can begin, the scope statement, the constraints and assumptions, and any other historical information must be reviewed to be certain that the work definition is correct and complete.

Activity Sequencing

The activity's identity comes from the work breakdown structure. When the WBS is completed, the bottom of the work breakdown structure defines the individual pieces of work necessary to complete the project. These individual pieces of work are the same items that become the activities in the project schedule. One of the things that is done in the development of the WBS is to check that each of the activities has inputs to do the work required. It is necessary that each output from an activity is used by another activity or is required as part of a project deliverable.

Dependencies can be categorized as mandatory, discretionary, and external and can be restricted by constraints and assumptions. Mandatory dependencies are those that are required as part of the nature of the work. These dependencies are sometimes called hard dependencies. The walls of a house cannot be built until the foundation is completed. Discretionary dependencies are those that are defined by management. There are preferred ways of doing things and may be determined by past experiences. External dependencies are those that are external to the project. These are all of the inputs that are supplied by anyone or anything outside the project.

Schedule Development & Control

Activity on Arrow Diagramming (AOA)

Activity on arrow diagramming is a network diagramming method that is seldom used today. However, there are a number of places where these can still be seen. Nearly all of the software programs that are available for project management have stopped using this diagramming method. We will discuss this method briefly since it still exists in the *Guide to the PMBOK.*

Activity on arrow diagrams can be recognized because the network diagram will always be shown with the activity information on the arrows instead of in the nodes of the diagram. The nodes of an activity on arrow diagram will always be shown as circles. This diagramming nomenclature is always followed.

Each activity in the diagram has two events associated with it. These events are of zero duration and are located at the beginning of the arrow and at the end of the arrow. This means that there are three things associated with each activity in the diagram, the activity description itself, the starting event of the activity, and the ending event of the activity.

The one advantage of this diagramming method is that, since the arrow is a line, the length of the line can be varied in proportion to the duration of the activity. This can be helpful in recognizing the magnitude of the duration of the activity. However, most management professionals feel that the complexity and difficulty in using this diagramming method is not compensated for by this ability.

Since the arrows in the diagram in Figure 5-1 represent the activities, it is necessary to create dummy activities to show multiple dependencies in the project being represented.

Calculations of schedules using this diagramming method are somewhat complicated than the precedence diagramming method, but the results will be the same.

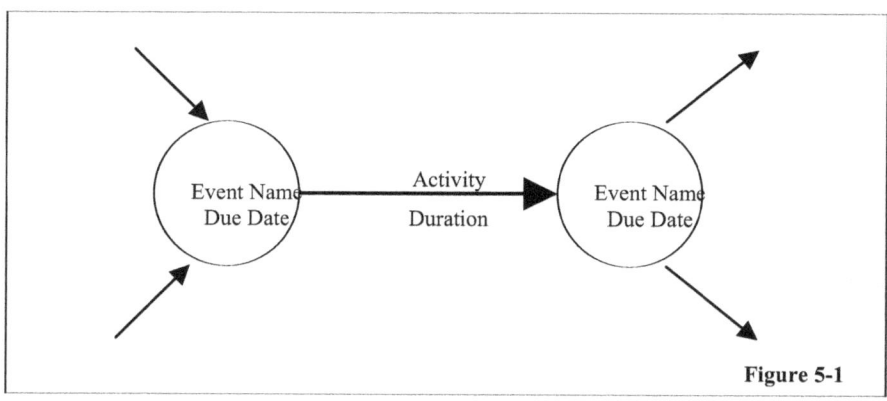

Figure 5-1

Precedence Diagramming Method (PDM)

Precedence diagramming is the method currently being used in nearly all of the project management software available today (Figure 5-2). This diagram is used to explain the mechanics of scheduling.

Precedence diagrams can be recognized because the network diagram is always shown with the activity information on the nodes instead of on the arrows of the diagram. The nodes of an activity in an arrow diagram will always be shown as rectangles. This diagramming form is always followed.

In its simplest form, the diagram contains boxes to indicate the activities in the schedule and arrows containing them. The boxes can contain any activity information that is desired, and project management software today has a great deal of flexibility in this regard. Today, all of this is done through the use of computer software for project management. The software allows you to annotate the boxes in the diagram with nearly any information you desire. Color and symbols can be used effectively to describe the diagram more fully.

The basic information that is normally included in the precedence diagram boxes is the activity number, description, early start, early finish, later start, late finish, and duration. The arrows connect the activities according to the logic that is required by the project. The arrows indicate the logical order that the activities may be worked on. The logic of the schedule can be considered as two activity pairs at a time. A pair of activities is any two (and only two) activities that are joined by an arrow. The tail (the part without the head) of the arrow indicates independent activity of the pair, and the head of the arrow indicates the dependent activity. Reading the diagram is easy if you keep this in mind and always consider the logical relationships of the network two activities at a time.

By saying that a relationship exists between two and only two activities, it does not mean that any activity cannot have more than one relationship. An activity might have two or more predecessors and it might have two or more successors (Figure 5-3).

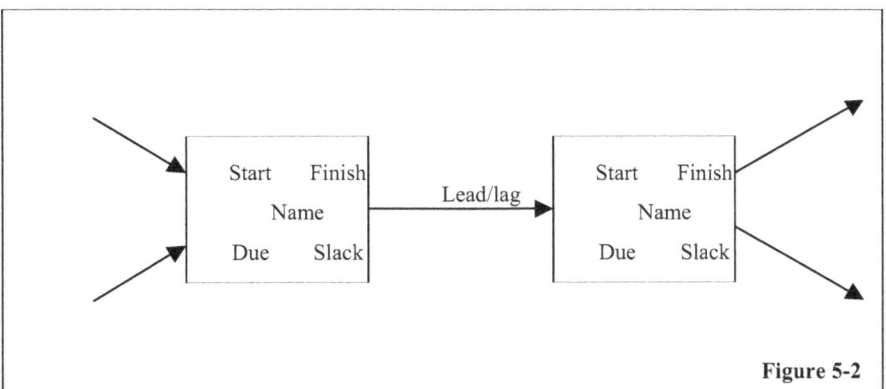

Figure 5-2

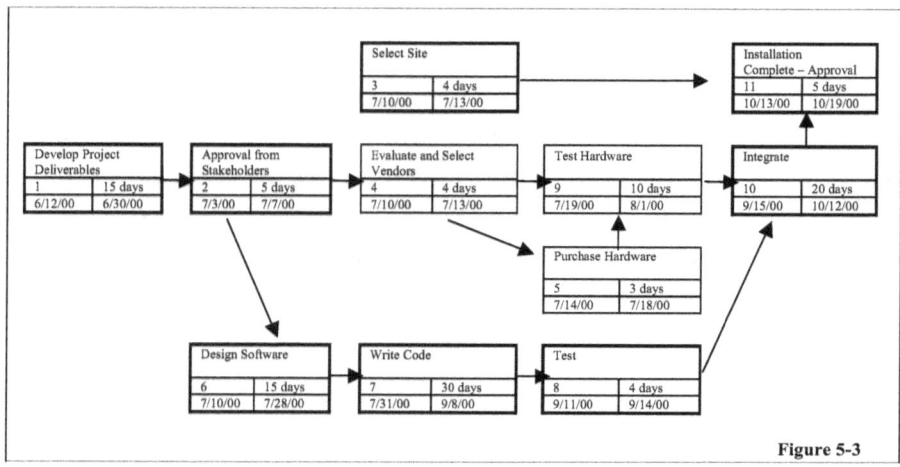

Figure 5-3

Logical Relationships

There are four possible logical relationships. You can remember these relationships if you use the same statement to describe the relationship and simply substitute the letters designating the relationship. The statement is: "The independent activity must (first letter of the relationship) before the dependent activity can (second letter of the relationship)" (Figure 5-4).

Finish-Start Relationship (FS): Most projects that you are likely to encounter use the logical relationship of finish-start more often than any other relationship. This relationship says: "The independent activity in the relationship must finish before the dependent activity can start".

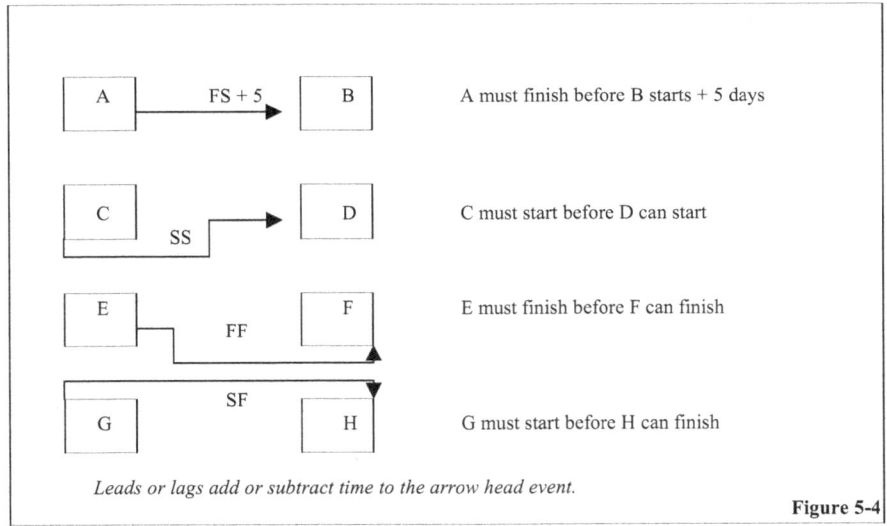

A — FS + 5 → B	A must finish before B starts + 5 days
C SS → D	C must start before D can start
E FF F	E must finish before F can finish
G SF H	G must start before H can finish

Leads or lags add or subtract time to the arrow head event.

Figure 5-4

This simply means that where there are two activities connected by an arrow, the one that is connected to the tail of the arrow must be finished before the activity connected to the head of the arrow is allowed to start. It does not say that the dependent activity must start then. The activity could start later than that time, but it is not allowed to start any sooner than the finish of the independent activity.

For example, we have two tasks to complete in our project. The project is to construct a wedding cake. The tasks are to make the cake and to on the frosting. The finish-start relationship says that we cannot start putting the frosting on the cake until we have baked the cake layers. Notice that we could, logically, put frosting on anytime after that. The relationship constricts the start of the activity of frosting the cake to be no sooner than the beginning of the master chef supervising the cake construction.

Finish-Finish Relationship (FF): The finish-finish relationship is expressed in the same way as the finish-start relationship except that the word finish is substituted for start. The relationship is stated like this:

"The independent activity in the relationship must finish before the dependent activity can finish".

This simply means that where there are two activities connected by an arrow; the one that is connected to the tail of the arrow must finish before the activity connected to the head of the arrow is allowed to finish. It does not say that the dependent activity must finish any sooner than the finish of the independent activity.

For example, we have two tasks to complete in my project. The project is to construct a wedding cake. The task in this example is to apply the frosting to the cake. We must have the master chef there until the frosting is complete so that he or she can approve it. The master chef is then restricted from finishing the supervising task until the frosting task is finished. The two tasks are applying frosting to the cake and the master chef supervising cake construction. The finish-finish relationship says that the master chef cannot finish supervising the cake construction until the frosting is completed. Notice that we could, logically, have the master chef continue supervising after that. The relationship constricts the finish of the master chef supervising activity to be no sooner than the finish of the frosting task.

Start-Finish Relationship (SF): The start-finish relationship is very seldom used and has been dropped from some of the project management software packages. The start-finish relationship is expressed in the same way as the finish-start relationship except that the words start and finish are substituted for finish and start. The relationship is started like this: "The independent activity in the relationship must start before the dependent activity can finish".

This simply says that where there are two activities connected by an arrow, the one that is connected to the tail of the arrow is allowed to finish. It does not say that the dependent activity must finish then. The dependent activity could finish later than that time, but it is not allowed to finish any sooner than the start of the independent activity.

For example, let us use the wedding cake project again. The task in this example is to apply the frosting to the cake until the master chef is on the scene. The two tasks then are to apply frosting to the cake and the master chef supervises cake construction. The start-start relationship says that we cannot start putting the frosting on the cake until the master chef is present. The start-finish relationship says that we can start putting on the frosting of the cake before the master chef is present, but we are not allowed to finish putting on the frosting until the master chef has started supervising. Notice that we could, logically, start putting frosting on anytime before the master chef begins to supervise. The relationship constricts the finish of the activity of frosting the cake to be no sooner than the beginning of the master chef supervising the cake construction.

Leads and Lags: Leads and lags are delays that are imposed in the relationship between the independent and dependent activity. Leads and lags can help to shorten schedules as well as allow for delays between activities. Leads and lags are designated by adding a plus for lags and a minus for leads and the number of time periods that the lead or lag adds to the schedule.

A lag causes the dependent activity of the pair of activities in the relationship to have the designated number of time periods added to the start or finish of the dependent activity. A lead causes the dependent activity of the pair of activities in the relationship to have the designated number of time periods subtracted from the start or finish of the dependent activity.

For example, in the two activities previously discussed, baking the cake and putting the frosting on the cake, we established a finish-start relationship between the two activities. This said that we could not apply the frosting until the cake was finished baking. This is all right if the baking of the cake activity ended when the cake was removed from the oven, then it would be necessary to insert a lag between the two activities. It is not a good idea to put the frosting on a hot cake, since it would melt and make a mess. But this may be necessary because the cake baker would like to have closure on the baking activity and go about doing other things, and we may want him to be responsible for waiting until the cake cools.

We change the relationship from an FS to an FS + 1. This forces the schedule to allow one time period between completion of the baking activity and the start of the frosting activity.

A lead, on the other hand, allows the dependent activity to start sooner than the logical relationship would normally allow. In the example showing the start-finish relationship, we wanted to show that the frosting activity could start sooner in this relationship than if we used a start-start relationship. The problem with the start-finish relationship is that the frosting activity could start very much earlier than the supervising activity. The result of this means that the person responsible for frosting the cake cannot get closure on the activity until the master chef arrives. Another way to show this relationship is to make an SS—1 relationship. This means that the frosting operation could start as early as one time period before the master chef arrives.

Diagramming Relationships

The convention used in network diagramming of relationships and leads and lags is that the relationship is shown on the logical arrow only if it is not a finish-start relationship. If there are no leads or lags, no designation is given.

Building the Network Diagram

A sequence of steps should be followed in developing the schedule:

1. Create a list of the activities that are to be scheduled.

2. Assign a duration to each of the activities.

3. Determine the predecessor for each activity.

4. Calculate the forward pass, the early schedule for each activity.

5. Calculate the backward pass, the late schedule for each activity.

6. Calculate the float for each activity.

7. Determine the critical path.

8. Determine if the predicted completion of the project is earlier than the promise date.

9. Adjust the schedule or the promise date.

10. Apply resources and determine resource constraints.

11. Adjust the schedule to allow for resource constraints.

12. Determine if the predicted project completion is earlier than the promise date.

13. Adjust the schedule or the promise date.

14. Get approval of the schedule.

Thus, the first thing we need to do is to create a list of activities that will be in our schedule. This list is identical to the bottom level of the work breakdown structure. The duration of each task was determined during the estimating process. The predecessor of each activity was determined during the final stages of the construction of the work breakdown structure.

Calculating the early schedule for each activity requires the adoption of a few scheduling conventions. These conventions are accepted by the scheduling community. The first activity is always scheduled to start on the project start date. This date is simply input as part of the project plan. The first start date is simply the project start. The early finish date is the early start date plus the duration of the activity. Another convention comes to play here. Each activity is considered to have started on the beginning of the start period and finishes at the end of the finish period. This means that if an activity has a duration of one day and it starts on January 1, it ends on January 1 as well. Due to this convention, the early finish of any activity equals the early start plus the duration minus one. So activity 1 starts on day 1 and finishes on day 15 (Figure 5-5).

The next activity must start in the beginning of the time period it starts in. This means that the next activity starts in the next available time period. Since activity one finishes on day 15, activity 2 must start on day 16 and finish on day 20.

Activities 3 and 4 present a new problem. Both of these activities depend on activity 2 to be completed before they can start. Both have an early start date of day 21. The schedule development continues, following the arrows.

In order to complete the backward pass, we must start at the last activity that was completed in the early schedule. The rationale for this is that if the early schedule was the soonest that the project could be completed, then we seek in the backward pass in the latest that each of the activities can be done so that the project can be completed.

We begin by taking the latest of the early finish times from the last activity to be completed. This is the late finish time. The duration is subtracted from the late finish time to get the early finish time. The late schedule times, late start and late finish for activity 11 are day 90 and day 94. Since activity 11 has a late start date of day 90, activity 10 and 3 must be finished no later than day 89. This is the late finish date for both of them. It is the latest that they can be finished in order to support the project completion of day 94 and the latest start of activity 11.

Remember the convention that says that the activity work always starts at the beginning of the work period and ends at the end of the work period. A late finish of day 94 and a duration of 5 days means that the activity must have started on day 90. Days 90, 91, 91, 93, and 94 are the five days worked. The durations are subtracted to get the late start dates for each activity. When we come to activity 2, we must be careful to choose a late finish date that supports the late start dates of activities 3, 4, and 6. Since the late start dates for activities 3, 4, and 6 are days 86, 53, and 21, respectively, the latest that activity 2 can be finished is day 20.

Now, if we refer to Figure 5-13, we will see that we have completed the calculation of the early start, early finish, late start, and late finish dates for our schedule.

Act	Description	Duration	Predecessor	ES	EF	LS	LF	Float
1	Develop project deliverables	15	–	1	15	1	15	0
2	Approval from stakeholders	5	1	16	20	16	20	0
3	Select site	4	2	21	24	86	89	65
4	Evaluate and select vendors	4	2	21	24	53	56	32
5	Purchase hardware	3	4	25	27	57	59	32
6	Design software	15	2	21	35	21	35	0
7	Write code	30	6	36	65	36	65	0
8	Test software	4	7	66	69	66	69	0
9	Test hardware	10	5	28	37	60	69	32
10	Integrate hardware & software	20	9, 8	70	89	70	89	0
11	Install and final acceptance	5	3, 10	90	94	90	94	0

Figure 5-5

When we calculated the early and late schedule dates for our project we found that in some of the dates the early and late schedule dates were the same and in other activities the dates were different. In these activities there was a difference between the earliest day that we could start an activity and the latest day we could start the activity. The difference between these two dates is called "float" or sometimes "slack". Either term means exactly the same thing, or they can be used interchangeably. The float of an activity is the amount of time that the activity can be delayed without causing a delay in the project.

To calculate the float for each task, subtract the early start day from the late start day of the activity. Incidentally, the subtraction could be performed using the late finish day and the early finish day as well, since the difference between start and finish dates is simply the duration, and that is the same for the early and late schedules.

Next, we determine the critical path. The critical path is really not a path at all. In the days when activity on arrow diagramming was used, the activities formed a path through the project schedule. Today, with the use of project management software, the critical path can be more versatile. The critical path is defined as the group of activities that cannot be delayed without delaying the completion date for the entire project. In other words, it is the series of activities that have "zero float".

Using project management software, the list of activities that are on the critical path can be modified to include activities that are nearly on the critical path. This is important, since the critical path is a management method for managing project schedules. The activities that have zero float are activities that cannot be delayed without delaying the completion of the project. These are the activities that must be monitored closely if we want our project to finish on time. Conversely, the activities that are not on the critical path, those activities have something other than zero float, need not be managed quite as closely. In addition, it is important to know which activities in the project may be delayed without delaying the project completion. Resources from activities having float could be made available to do a work around if the need should arise.

Now that we have determined our schedule for the earliest completion of the project, it is time for a reality check. We must determine if predicted project completion is less than promise date. The schedule should be showing a completion date that is earlier than the promise date that may have already been given to the stakeholders. If this is not the case, then warning flags should be up and waving.

The schedule that we have produced so far has not yet included delays that will occur if resources are not available when they are needed. Schedule reserves have not yet been added to allow for the effect of known and unknown risks. We also have not taken into consideration the normal variations that will occur between the predicted and actual project activity durations.

Next, we need to adjust the schedule or the promise date. We have two situations, a schedule that has a promise date that is earlier than the predicted date and a schedule that has a promise date that is later than the predicted date. If the predicted date of the schedule is later than the promise date, crashing or fast tracking must be used. Crashing a schedule is doing anything at all to reduce the schedule completion of the project. Examples of crashing include reducing the scope of the project, adding additional resources to selected activities, eliminating activities, and changing the process to eliminate steps.

Fast tracking is a special case of crashing. In fast tracking, activities that would have been scheduled in sequence are scheduled to be done with some overlap instead. The use of leads in the logical relationships between activities can be used to facilitate this, or the relationships can be changed completely.

The project is to paint a building (Figure 5-6). The original schedule called for one crew of people to scrape off the loose paint, apply the primer, and then apply the finish coat. The schedule called for the three activities to be done in sequence.

To improve on the scheduled completion of the project, some of the activities could be fast tracked. Instead of one crew, two crews could be utilized. The first crew starts chipping and scraping. Eight hours later the second crew starts applying the primer. When the first crew finishes scraping and chipping the building, they can begin painting the finish coat over the primer that the second crew has been applying (Figure 5-7).

The overall effect is to reduce the time for doing the project from 30 hours to 22 hours. The work content, or the effort, remains the same at 30 person-hours. If the crew size were 2 people, then the project effort would be 60 person-hours. The disadvantage of fast tracking the schedule as we have done here is the cost or risk or both increases.

In this example, the overall cost of the project did not go up according to what we have measured. However, the real cost of the project, of all things are considered, has gone up. Transportation of the additional crew to the job site increases the cost. The cost of additional equipment needed to equip two crews has increased.

The risk of the project goes up as well. If a mistake is made by one crew or the other, there will be little time to recover before the project schedule is affected. If a mistake is made, for example, the wrong primer is used, the finish coat may have already been applied before the mistake is discovered (Figure 5-7).

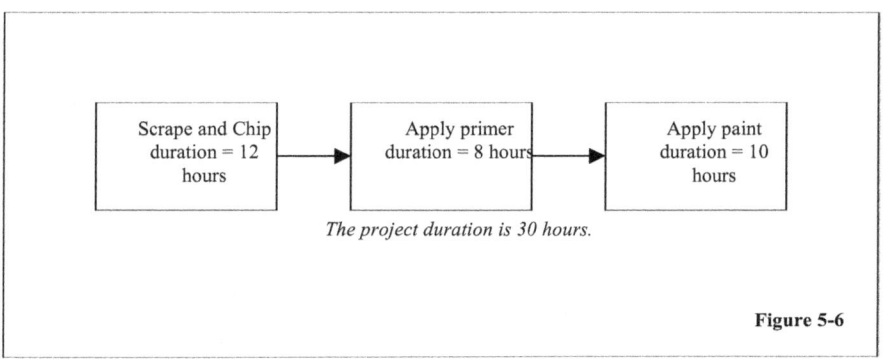

The project duration is 30 hours.

Figure 5-6

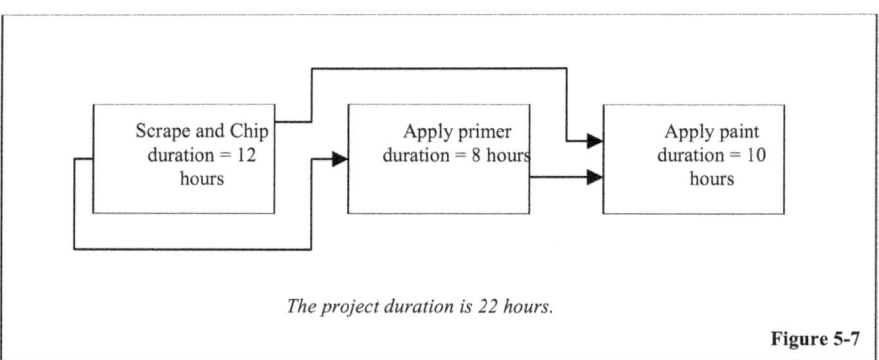

The project duration is 22 hours.

Figure 5-7

Buffering the Schedule: The order problem that we must address is what to do if the schedule is less than the promise date of the project to the stakeholders. This is a much more pleasant problem than trying to shorten the schedule. It is an important problem to solve, however.

We need to check to see if the schedule has been calculated is less than the promise date. This must be done after allowing for reserve schedule time, normal fluctuations in the activity durations, and resource limitations (Figure 5-8). If after all of this the schedule time is less than the promise date, buffering may be applied.

A project schedule should not be adjusted by lengthening the duration of the activities (Figure 5-9). If this is done, each of the people responsible for a scheduled activity is essentially given the extra allowance and will probably work to this schedule. The schedule should also not be left as it was since this is an optimistic schedule with no allowances for the items we discussed earlier.

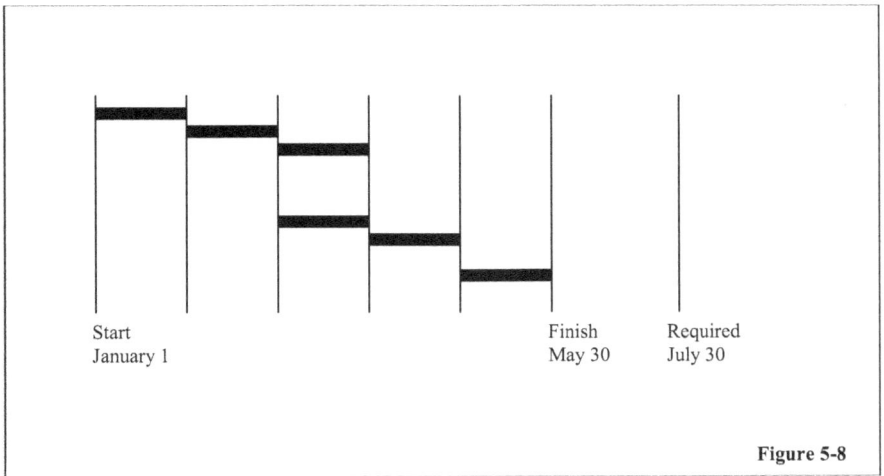

Start
January 1

Finish
May 30

Required
July 30

Figure 5-8

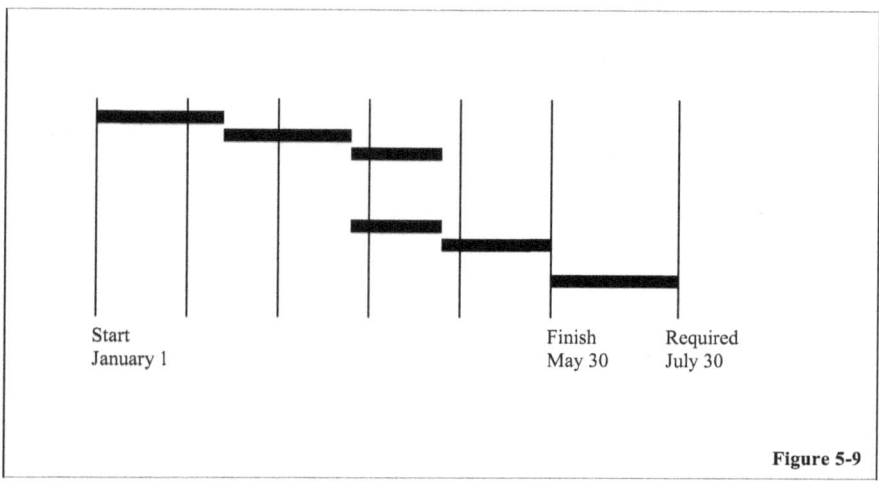

Start
January 1

Finish
May 30

Required
July 30

Figure 5-9

A better way to schedule the project is with a buffer (Figure 5-10). Buffering a schedule is simply adding float to selected activities. In some project management software this feature is available. If it is not it can still be done by using lags in the relationships and creating buffer activities.

Using relationship lags is easily done but is tedious to accomplish. Each pair of tasks must be considered and a lag added wherever it is desired to add buffer. To increase the project's scheduled completion, a lag may be added between any two activities on the critical path. Changing the relationship from a normal finish-start to an FS + 10 would add ten days of float to the activity and also shift the project completion to ten days later.

Another technique is to create a duplicate activity for each activity that is to be buffered (Figure 5-11). The activity created is inserted between the independent activity to be buffered and the dependent activity in the relationship. If there was originally as FS relationship between A and B, the new relationship would add activity Á. This gives us an FS relationship between A and Á and another between Á and B. When this technique is used, the buffering dummy activities can be selected out of the schedule so that they will not appear. The remaining activities in the schedule will show with their correct dates.

Which activities should be buffered? This can be answered in a number of ways. The amount of buffer time that is applied to activities can be proportioned according to the risk of the activity, the dependencies that follow it, or any other reason that seems appropriate to the project manager.

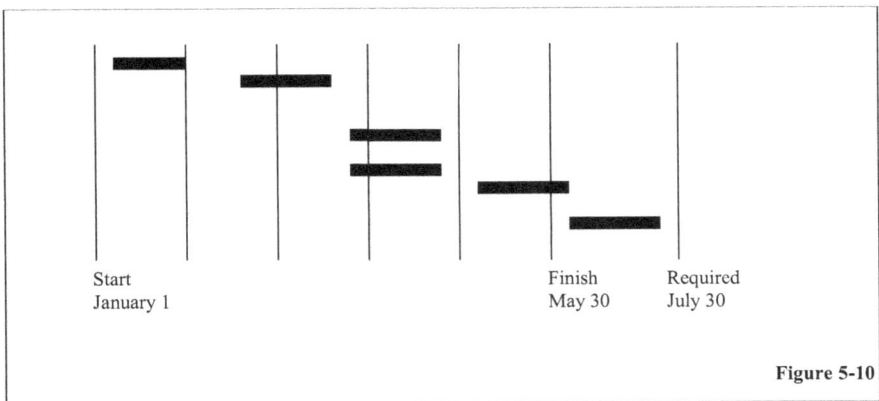

Start
January 1

Finish
May 30

Required
July 30

Figure 5-10

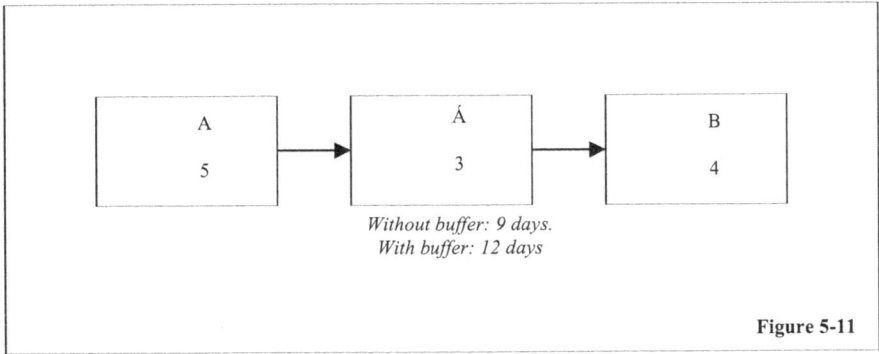

Without buffer: 9 days.
With buffer: 12 days

Figure 5-11

In all project management software available today there is the ability to constrain the project with the use of resource. The unavailability of resources may cause schedule delays. This problem occurs when a task is scheduled that uses a particular person or equipment and that person or piece of equipment is being used in some other part of the project or on some other project altogether.

Critical Path Method (CPM)

The CPM is a method of managing a project effectively. We have seen how the critical path is determined and how the float or slack is determined. Using the notion of float, the project manager can direct his or her efforts where they will do the most good.

Activities that are found to have float, particularly those that have larger amounts of float, can be managed less intensely than other activities in the project plan. This is because activities with float can be delayed without affecting the project completion date. Of course, activities that have large amounts of float can be delayed a considerable amount before they affect the project completion (Figure 5-12).

Conversely, the activities that have zero float cannot be delayed without affecting the project completion date. These activities should be managed carefully by the project manager and the project team.

In the critical path method of managing projects another term for float is free float. This is somewhat different than the float we have discussed up until now. One of the problems with managing by float is that if an activity can be is delayed within its float, it may be necessary to reschedule many other activities as a result. Free float is the amount of time an activity can be delayed without affecting the project completion date or requiring any other activity to be rescheduled. This is important, because rescheduling the remaining activities in the project can cause great confusion for the project team members, and the project manager can quickly lose credibility. The use of free float prevents much of this problem.

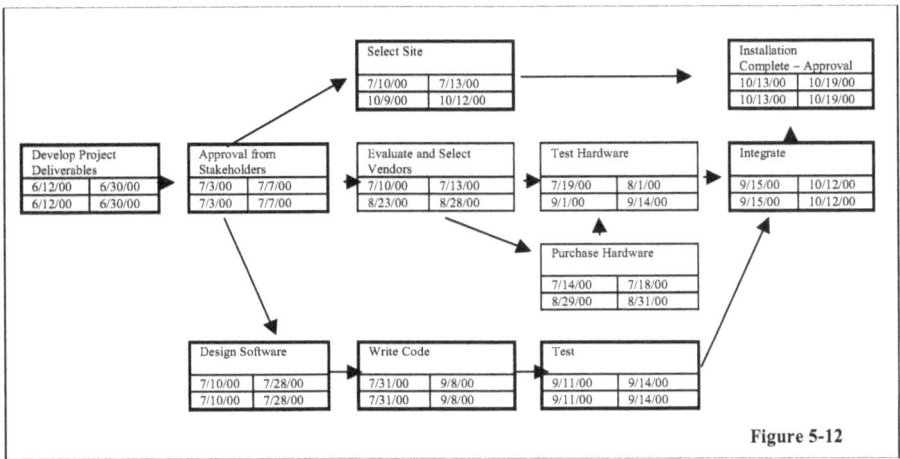

Figure 5-12

Program Evaluation and Review Technique (PERT)

The PERT system was developed for the Polaris Missile Program the 1950s. At this time there was a lot of pressure on the United States Navy to complete the Polaris Missile Program. The Cold War was raging, and the United States needed a deterrent that would discourage the threat of nuclear war with the Soviet Union. A mobile missile that could be carried aboard a submarine and launched from beneath the surface of the sea would be a formidable weapon.

The problem for the Navy was that there were two separate projects to be done. One was to develop a submarine that could launch these missiles. The second project was to develop a missile that could be launched from a submarine. The durations of the project plan activities had a great deal of uncertainty in them. The Navy needed a method to predict the project schedule with better reliability than was possible in the past. PERT was developed to assist in analyzing projects where there was uncertainty about the duration of the tasks.

The normal probability distribution relates the event of something happening to the probability that it will occur. It turns out that by experiment, the normal distribution describes many phenomena that actually occur. The duration as well as the estimated cost of project activities comes close to matching a normal distribution. In reality, another distribution, called the beta distribution, fits these phenomena better, but the normal curve is close enough for practical purposes.

In Figure 5-12, we have a schedule that has as expected completion time of 94 days (Figure 5-13). Since 94 days is the expected value of the project, it follows that it would have the highest probability of all of the other possibilities. Another way of saying this is that if all of the possibilities are shown, then they represent 100 percent of the possibilities and 100 percent of the probability.

If it were possible for a project to be done thousands of times, sometimes the time to do the schedule would be 94 days, other times it would be 93 days, and still other times it would be 97 days. If we were to plot all of these experiments we would find that 94 days occurred most often, 93 days occurred a little less than often, 92 days even less, and so on. Experimentally we could develop a special probability distribution for this particular activity. The curve would then describe the probability that any particular duration would occur when we really decided to do the project and that task. In the experiment, if 94 days occurred 134 times and the experiment was performed 1,000 times, we could say that there is a 13.4 percent chance that the actual doing of the project would take 94 days. All 1,000 of the activity times were between 78 and 110 days.

It is impractical to do this when we schedule it. If we are willing to agree that many phenomena, such as schedule durations and cost, will fit the normal probability distribution, then we can avoid doing the experiment and instead do the mathematics. In order to do this, we only need to have a simple way to approximate the mean and standard deviation of the phenomena.

The mean value is the middle of the curve along the x-axis. This is the average or expected value. A good approximation of this value can be obtained by asking the activity estimator to estimate three values instead of the usual one. We must ask the estimator to estimate the optimistic, the pessimistic, and the most likely. The way people perform estimating function is to think about what will happen if things go well, what will happen if things do not go well, and then what is likely to happen. Thus, these are the optimistic, the pessimistic, and the most likely value for the activity duration.

If we have these three values, it becomes simple to calculate the expected value and the standard deviation. For the expected value we will take the weighted average:

Expected Value = [Optimistic + Pessimistic + (4 x Most likely)] ÷ 6

Standard Deviation = (Pessimistic—Optimistic) ÷ 6

Act	Description	Optimistic	Pessimistic	Most Likely	EV	SD	Variance	CP EV	CP Variance
1	Develop project deliverables	13	16	15	14.83	0.50	0.2500	14.83	0.0625
2	Approval from stakeholders	4	6	5	5.00	0.33	0.1111	5.00	0.0123
3	Select site	4	4	4	4.00	0.00	0.0000		
4	Evaluate and select vendors	4	5	4	4.17	0.17	0.0278		
5	Purchase hardware	3	3	3	3.00	0.00	0.0000		
6	Design software	14	17	15	15.17	0.50	0.2500	15.17	0.0625
7	Write code	24	33	30	29.50	1.50	2.2500	29.50	5.0625
8	Test software	4	4	4	4.00	0.00	0.0000	4.00	0.0000
9	Test hardware	9	11	10	10.00	0.33	0.1111		
10	Integrate hardware & software	20	23	20	20.50	0.50	0.2500	20.50	0.0625
11	Install and final acceptance	5	5	5	5.00	0.00	0.0000	5.00	0.0000
					Sum =			94.00	5.2623

Figure 5-13

With these two simple calculations we can calculate the probability and a range of values that the dates for the completion of the project will have when we actually do the project. For the purpose of ease of calculation, if we were to decide that 95.5 percent probability would be sufficient for our purposes, than it turns out that this happens to be the range of values that is plus or minus 2 standard deviations from the mean value.

If the expected value of the schedule was 94 days and the standard deviation was 2.3 days we could make the statement: "This project has a probability of 95 percent that it will finish between 89.4 and 98.3 days".

Monte Carlo Simulation

When a schedule with activities that have uncertainty associated with their durations is encountered, the PERT method can be used to help predict the probability and range of values that will encompass the actual duration of the project.

While the PERT technique uses the normal and beta distributions to determine this probability and range of values, there is a serious flaw in the results. The assumption made in the PERT analysis is that the critical path of the project remains the same under any of the possible conditions. This is, of course, a dangerous assumption. In any given set of possibilities, it is quite possible that the critical path may shift from one set of activities to another, thus, changing the predicted completion date of the project.

In order to predict the project completion date when there is a possibility that the critical path will be different for a given set of project conditions, the Monte Carlo simulation must be used. The Monte Carlo simulation is a simulation not a deterministic method like many of the tools that we normally use. By that we mean that there is no exact solution that will come from the Monte Carlo analysis. What we will get instead is a probability distribution of the possible days for the project completion.

Monte Carlo simulations have been around for some time and they are offered in most of project management software packages. It is only recently that project management software packages have become inexpensive for many project managers to afford.

The Simulation: In our project schedule, the predecessors and successors form a critical path. The critical path is the list of activities in the project schedule that cannot be delayed without affecting the completion date of the project. These are the activities that have zero float. Float is the number of days an activity can be delayed without affecting the completion date of the project.

When we have uncertainty in the duration times for the activities in the schedule it means that there is at least a possibility that the activity will take more time or less time than our most likely estimate. If we used PERT to make these calculations, we already have calculated the mean value and the standard deviation for the project and all of the activities that have uncertainty.

The Monte Carlo simulator randomly selects values that are the possible durations for each of the activities having possible different durations. The selection of a duration for each activity is made, and the calculation of the project completion date is made for that specific set of data. The critical path is calculated as well as the overall duration and completion date for the project.

The simulator usually allows for the selection of several probability distributions. This can be done for one activity, a group of activities, or the entire project. Depending on the software package being used, a selection of probability distributions is offered, such as: uniform, binominal, triangular, Poisson, beta, normal, and others.

The Monte Carlo simulation works in a step-by-step way:

1) A range of values is determined for the duration of each activity in the schedule that has uncertainty in its duration.

2) A probability distribution is selected for each activity or group of activities.

3) If necessary, the mean and standard deviation are calculated for each activity.

4) The network relationships between the activities are entered.

5) The computer simulation is begun.

6) A duration time is selected for each activity in the schedule, whether on the critical path or not.

7) The critical path, duration of the project, float, and other schedule data are calculated.

8) This process is repeated many times until the repetitions reach a certain predefined number of cycles or until the results reach a certain accuracy.

9) Output reports are generated.

Output from the Monte Carlo Simulation: The most common output from Monte Carlo simulation is a chart showing the probability of each possible completion date. This is usually shown as a frequency histogram. Generally, a cumulative plot is made as well. In this way we may see graphically the probability of each of the possible dates. This clearly shows the most likely dates for project completion. Because of the shifting the critical path, it is quite possible for early dates and late dates to be the most likely, with unlikely dates in between them.

A cumulative curve is also produced that shows the cumulative probability of completing before a given date. The criticality index can be calculated. This is the percentage of the time that a particular activity is on the critical path. In other words, if a simulation ran 1,000 times and particular activity was on the critical path 212 times, its criticality index would be 21.2 percent.

6

Cost Management

Resource Planning
Project Life Cycle and Project Cost
Cost Estimating
Cost Budgeting
Cost Control

Cost Management

Cost management is the completion of the project management triple constraint of cost, schedule, and scope. Each of these must be completed in order to complete the project on time and within the budget and meet all of the customer's expectations. In order to meet the cost goals of the project, the project must be completed within the approved budget.

Purpose of Cost Management: The project manager is primarily concerned with the direct cost of the project, but the trend in project management is that the role of the project manager in cost control will increase to include more of the nontraditional areas of cost control. In the future it will be expected that more project managers will have a great deal of input into the indirect costs and expenses of the project.

Regardless of what the project manager is or is not responsible for, it is critical that the project be measured against what the project manager is responsible for and nothing else. If the project manager does not have responsibility for material cost of the project, then it makes no sense for the project manager to be measured against this matrix.

Timing of the collection of cost information is also important to the cost measurement system. The project budgets must be synchronized with the collection of the project's actual cost. For example, if a project team is responsible for material cost, should the budget show the expenditure when the commitment by the project team to buy the product is made, when the item is delivered, when it is accepted, or when it is paid for? Timing issues like these can make project cost control a nightmare.

If the project team does not properly control cost, the project will invariably go out of control, and more money will be spent than anticipated. It is the purpose of cost management to prevent this action.

Resource Planning

Resource planning involves determining what physical resources (e.g., people, materials, equipment, etc.) and what quantities of each should be used and when they would be needed to perform project activities. It must be closely coordinated with cost estimating. For example:

- A construction project team will need to be familiar with local building codes. Such knowledge is often readily available from local sellers. However, if the local labor pool lacks experience with unusual or specialized construction techniques, the additional cost for a consultant might be the most effective way to secure knowledge of the local building codes.

- An automotive design team should be familiar with the latest in automated assembly techniques. The requisite knowledge might be obtained by hiring a consultant, by sending a designer to a seminar on robotics, or by including someone from manufacturing as a member of the team.

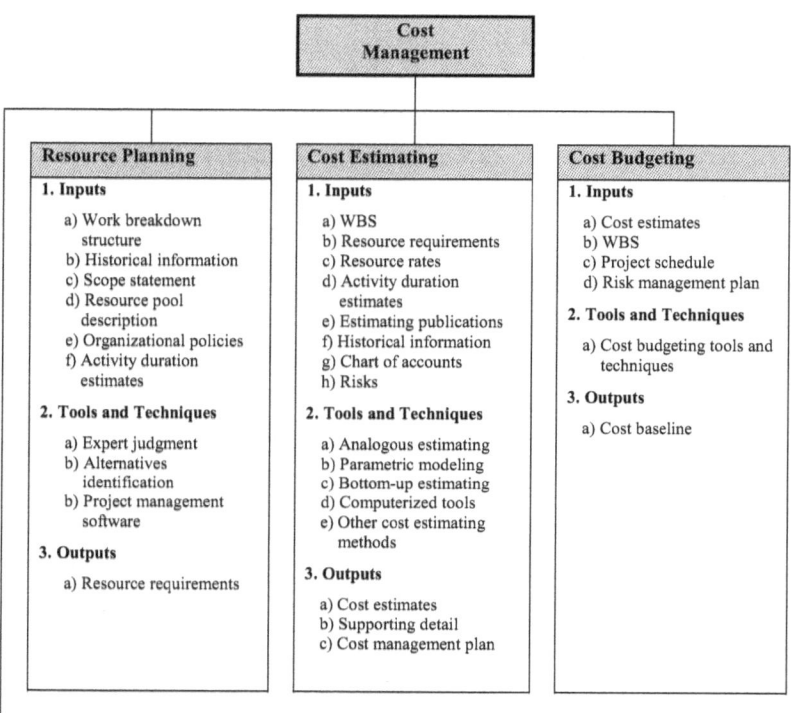

Cost Management

Resource Planning

1. Inputs
   a) Work breakdown structure
   b) Historical information
   c) Scope statement
   d) Resource pool description
   e) Organizational policies
   f) Activity duration estimates

2. Tools and Techniques
   a) Expert judgment
   b) Alternatives identification
   b) Project management software

3. Outputs
   a) Resource requirements

Cost Estimating

1. Inputs
   a) WBS
   b) Resource requirements
   c) Resource rates
   d) Activity duration estimates
   e) Estimating publications
   f) Historical information
   g) Chart of accounts
   h) Risks

2. Tools and Techniques
   a) Analogous estimating
   b) Parametric modeling
   c) Bottom-up estimating
   d) Computerized tools
   e) Other cost estimating methods

3. Outputs
   a) Cost estimates
   b) Supporting detail
   c) Cost management plan

Cost Budgeting

1. Inputs
   a) Cost estimates
   b) WBS
   c) Project schedule
   d) Risk management plan

2. Tools and Techniques
   a) Cost budgeting tools and techniques

3. Outputs
   a) Cost baseline

Cost Control

1. Inputs
   a) Cost baseline
   b) Performance reports
   c) Change requests
   d) Cost management plan

2. Tools and Techniques
   a) Cost change control system
   b) Performance measurement
   c) Earned value management (EVM)
   d) Additional planning
   e) Computerized tools

3. Outputs
   a) Revised cost estimates
   b) Budget updates
   c) Corrective action
   d) Estimate at completion
   e) Project closeout
   Lessons learned

Figure 6-1

Project Life Cycle & Project Cost

Lately, it has become important to consider the cost of the project for the full useful life of the product or service that is created. This means that the cost of the project does not end when final acceptance of the project has been completed. Guaranties, warranties, and ongoing services that must be performed during the life of the project must be considered.

With regard to project life cycle, cost decisions are made with a clearer picture of the future commitments that the project will require. If life cycle cost is considered, better decisions will be made. An example of this is creating a software program for a customer. The project team can create a working software program without organization or documentation. This is usually called "spaghetti code". Considering The cost of the project as delivered, the "spaghetti coded" project will be less costly. Considering the life cycle cost of the project, however, this approach is more costly. This is because the cost of debugging and modifying the software after delivery of the project will be more difficult.

Using the Work Breakdown Structure: The WBS is the key to successful projects. The work breakdown structure produces a list of the individual pieces of work that must be done to complete a project. These are the building blocks of the project. Each of these represents a portion of the work of the project. Each of them must be the responsibility of one and only one person on the project team. The person responsible for an individual piece of work is similar to the project manager and is responsible for all that happens in the project regarding that piece of work. That person is responsible for scheduling, cost estimating, time estimating, and seeing that the work gets done. Like the project manager, the person responsible may not be required to do all the work. He or she is, however, responsible for seeing that it gets done.

As you have noticed, I have been using the phrase "individual piece of work" to describe the bottom level of the WBS. This is because the PMI make some distinctions between terms. These individual pieces of work can be referred to as work packages, tasks, or activities. Most project managers would not make a distinction between these three terms, and if they did, the meanings would probably be different among project managers. Most project managers at least use the words *activity* and *task* interchangeably.

The *Guide to the PMBOK* definition is: a work package is the lowest level of the WBS. This means that it is the lowest level that the project manager intends to manage to. In a very large project with a hierarchical structure of project managers and subproject managers, there will be managers for the work packages, and each manager will have his or her own work breakdown structure. Eventually a point is reached where cost, resources, and duration define the individual pieces of work. These, according to the *Guide to the PMBOK*, are called activities. Activities may be further subdivided into tasks. Learning all this may get you a point on the PMP exam, but for our purposes in this text we will use the terms *activity* and *task* interchangeably.

In order to determine the project cost accurately enough to be considered the project cost baseline, a bottom-up estimate must be made. This estimate must have an accuracy of -5 percent and +10 percent. This type of estimate will be produced by estimating the cost of each item at the bottom level of the WBS and then summarizing or rolling up the data to the project level.

Bottom-up estimates are inherently more accurate because they are a sum of individual elements. Each of the individual elements has a possibility of being over or under the actual cost that will occur. When they are added together, some of the overestimates will cancel out some if the underestimates.

Cost Estimating

A cost estimate is a prediction of the likely cost of the resources that will be required to complete all of the work of the project.

Cost estimating is done throughout the project. In the beginning of the project proof of concept estimates must be done to allow the project to go on. An "order of magnitude" estimate is performed at this stage of the project. Order-of-magnitude estimates can have an accuracy of -25 percent to +75 percent. As the project progresses, more accurate estimates are required. Budget estimates are those that have an accuracy of -10 percent to +25 percent. Finally, at the time of creating the project cost baseline, the definitive estimate is 5 to 10 percent. Early in the project there is much uncertainty about what is actually to be done in the project. There is no point in expending the effort to make a more accurate estimate than the accuracy needed at the particular stage that the project is in.

There are several types of estimates in common use. Depending on the accuracy required for the estimate and the cost and effort that can be expended there are several choices.

Top-Down Estimates: Top-down estimates are used to estimate cost early in the project when information about the project is very limited. Top-down comes from the idea that the estimate is made at the top level of the project. That is, the project itself is estimated with one single estimate. The advantage of this type of estimate is that it requires much less effort and requires very little time to produce. The disadvantage is that the accuracy of the estimate is not as good as it would be with a more detailed estimating effort.

Bottom-up Estimates: Bottom-up estimates are used when the project baselines are required or a definitive type of estimate is needed. These types of estimates are called bottom up because they begin by estimating the details of the project and then summarizing the details into summary levels. The WBS can be used for this "roll up". The advantage of this kind of estimate is that it will produce accurate results. The accuracy of the bottom-up estimate depends on the level of detail that is considered. Statistically, convergence takes place as more and more detail is added. The disadvantage of this type of estimate is that the cost of doing detailed estimating is higher, and the time to produce the estimate is considerably longer.

Analogous Estimates: Analogous estimates are a form of top-down estimate. This process uses the actual cost of previously completed projects to predict the cost of the project that is being estimated. Thus, there is an analogy between one project and another. If the project being used in the analogy and the project being estimated are very similar, the estimates could be quite accurate. If the projects are not very similar, then the estimates might not be very accurate at all.

For example, a new software development project is to be done. The modules to be designed are very similar to modules that were used on another project but the current modules require more lines of code. The difficulty of the project is quite similar to the previous project. If the new project is 30 percent larger than the previous project, the analogy might predict a project cost of 30 percent greater than that of the previous project.

Parametric Estimates: Parametric estimates are similar to analogous estimates in that they are also top-down estimates. Their inherent accuracy is no better or worse than analogous estimates.

The process of parametric estimating is accomplished by finding a parameter of the project being estimated that changes proportionately with project cost. A mathematical model is built based on one or more parameters. When the values of the parameters are entered into the model, the cost of the project results.

If there is a close relationship between the parameters and cost and the parameters are easy to quantify, the accuracy can be improved. If there are historical projects that are both more costly and less costly than the project being estimated and the parametric relationship is true for both of those historical projects, the estimating accuracy and the reliability of the parameter for this project will be better.

Multiple parameter estimates can be produced as well. In multiple parameter estimates, various weights are given to each parameter to allow for the calculation of cost by several parameters simultaneously. For example, houses cost $115 per square foot. Software development cost is $2 per line of code produced. An office building is $254 per square foot plus $54 per cubic foot plus $2000 per acre of land.

Definitive Estimates: Definitive estimates are of the bottom-up variety. This is the type of estimate that is used to establish a project baseline or any other important estimate. In a project, the WBS can be used as a level of detail for the estimate. The accuracy of this estimate can be made to be quite high, but the cost of developing the estimate can be quite high and the time to produce it can be lengthy as well.

Definitive estimates are based on the statistical central limit theorem, which explains statistical convergence. If we have a group of details that can be summarized, the variance of the sum of the details will be less significant than the significance of the variance of the details themselves. All this means is that the more details we have in an estimate, the more accurate the sum of the details will be, because some of the estimates of the details will be overestimated and some will be underestimated. The overestimates and underestimates will cancel each other out. If we have enough detail, the average overestimates and underestimates will approach a zero difference.

If we flip the coin one time, it comes up 100 percent heads or 100 percent tails. If we continue flipping the coin a large number of times, and the coin is a fair coin, then 50 percent of the flips will be heads and 50 percent of the flips will be tails. It may be that there are more heads than tails at one time or another, but if we flip the coin long enough, there will be 50 percent heads and 50 percent tails at the end of the coin flipping.

If we know the mean or expected values and the standard deviations for a group of detailed estimates, we can calculate the expected value and the standard deviation of the sum. If we are also willing to accept that the probability of the estimate being correct follows a normal probability distribution, then we can predict the range of values and the probability of the actual cost.

Using the same estimates for the expected value and the standard deviation that we used in the PERT method for schedules, we can make these calculations. There are only approximations of these values, but they are close enough to be used in our estimating work.

Expected Value = (Optimistic + Pessimistic + [4 × Most Likely]) ÷ 6

Standard Deviation = (Pessimistic—Optimistic) ÷ 6

Where do these values come from? Most estimators report a single value when they complete a cost estimate. However, they think about what the cost will be if things go badly, and they think about what the cost will be if things go well. These thoughts that they have are really the optimistic and pessimistic values that we need for our calculations. They do not cost us a thing to get. All we have to do is to get the estimator to report them to us.

For definitive estimates we are usually happy to get a 5 percent probability of being correct. As luck would have it, this happens to be the range of values that is plus or minus two standard deviations from the mean or expected value.

For example, suppose we want to estimate the cost of a printed circuit board for a electrical device of some sort. In Figure 6-2, the optimistic, pessimistic, and most likely values that were estimated are entered in column 2, 3, and 4. From these estimated values the expected value of the individual components can be calculated. This is shown in column 5. The expected value of the assembly can be reached by adding the expected values.

The standard deviation for each component is calculated and shown in column 6. In order to add the standard deviations they must first be squared. These values are shown in column 7. Next, the square of each of the standard deviations for each component is added and the square root is taken of the total. This is the standard deviation of the assembly.

The expected value of the assembly is $5.54, and the standard deviation is 7.3 cents. We are interested in the range of values that have a probability of containing the actual cost if the assembly when it is produced. The range of values that has a 95 percent probability of occurring is plus or minus two standard deviations from the expected value.

In our example we can say that the assembly has a 95 percent probability of costing between $5.39 and $5.67.

Item	Description	Optimistic	Pessimistic	Most Likely	Expected Value	Standard Deviation	SD Squared
1	100 ohm resistor	0.04	0.06	0.05	0.050	0.0033	0.00001089
2	200 ohm resistor	0.06	0.09	0.07	0.072	0.0050	0.00002500
3	10 ohm resistor	0.03	0.04	0.03	0.032	0.0017	0.00000289
4	10 mf capacitor	0.22	0.25	0.22	0.225	0.0050	0.00002500
5	20 mf capacitor	0.28	0.36	0.33	0.327	0.0133	0.00017689
6	5 mf capacitor	0.11	0.13	0.12	0.120	0.0033	0.00001089
7	Integrated circuit	1.66	1.88	1.79	1.783	0.0367	0.00134689
8	Wire	0.33	0.33	0.33	0.330	0.0000	0.00000000
9	Circuit board	1.70	2.05	1.98	1.945	0.0583	0.00339889
10	Connector	0.57	0.70	0.67	0.658	0.0217	0.00047089
						Sum of Squares:	0.00546823
				Total Cost:	5.542	Standard Deviation:	0.07394748

Cost Budgeting

Cost budgeting the process of allocating cost to the individual work items in the project. Project performance will be determined based on the budget allocated to the various parts of the project. The result of the cost budgeting process is the cost baseline of the project.

The cost baseline for the project is the expected actual cost of the project. The budget for a project should contain the estimated cost of doing all of the work that is planned to be done for the project to be completed. In addition to the work that is required for completing the planned work of the project, cost must be budgeted for work that will be done to avoid, transfer, and mitigate risks. Contingency must be budgeted for risks that are identified and may or may not come to pass. A reserve must be budgeted for risks that are not identified.

On most projects, the expected value for risks is budgeted. This is reasonable since it reflects the average risk exposure for the project. Using the worst case situation or the best case situation for the project would be overly pessimistic or optimistic.

Cost Control

Cost control is the process of controlling the project cost and taking corrective action when the control indicates that corrective action is necessary.

Earned Value Management (EVM): The earned value management is a reporting system which is now the most commonly used method of performance measurement and project control. The reason for the popularity of this reporting system in project management is that is includes performance to cost and performance to schedule in one report. Schedule and cost are both measured in dollars. Where EVM is not used, reports favor measuring performance to schedule or performance to budget.

In any reporting system the principle is to set some standard and then measure the actual performance to that standard and report on the observed differences. In the EVM reporting system we use the planned budget and schedule and then measure the actual progress in the budget and schedule.

Frequently, the Gantt charts (bar charts) are used to show progress and performance to schedule, but this does not state the case clearly. If a scheduled activity is shown to be three days behind schedule, it is important to know if there is one person involved in this activity or if there are twenty.

In reporting cost, actual cost is frequently compared to budget cost to date. This does not show the full picture either. If a project is behind schedule, the actual cost could be tracking nicely to the expected budgeted expenditures, and the project could still be in a great deal of trouble.

Using the EVM reporting system the progress of the project in terms of cost is measured in dollars. The progress of the project in terms of schedule is also measured in dollars. This may sound confusing to people who are used to thinking of schedule in terms of days ahead or behind. In fact it is a more informational description of the condition of the project schedule. If a project activity is reported as being five days behind schedule, and there is one person working on the activity part time, it is very different than an activity that is behind five days that has twenty people working on it full time.

Obviously, what is needed is a reporting system that combines performance, schedule, and budget. This is the purpose of the earned value management system.

Cumulative Reporting: Earned value management reports (EVM) are cumulative reports. The values collected for the current reporting period are added to the values from the last reporting period, and the total is plotted.

Cumulative values will never go down unless a value is reversed. It can be seen in Figure 6-3 that cumulative cost curves have a characteristic "S" shape. This is because typically project teams start out spending money slowly and gradually increase their spending rate until a peak is reached and then gradually decrease their rate of spending until the project is finally completed.

One difficulty in showing the cumulative cost curve for a larger project is that the scale required to show the entire cost of the project may be so compact that relatively large variations are not visible. A $400 million project plotted on an 8 ½- by-11-inch page has a million dollar variation shown by one-fiftieth of an inch.

Where large numbers are used, a plot of the variance can be used. The scale of this type of chart can be much less compact and still show the needed information. It is made by simply drawing a line as a zero base and then plotting the difference between actual and expected values, as illustrated in Figure 6-4.

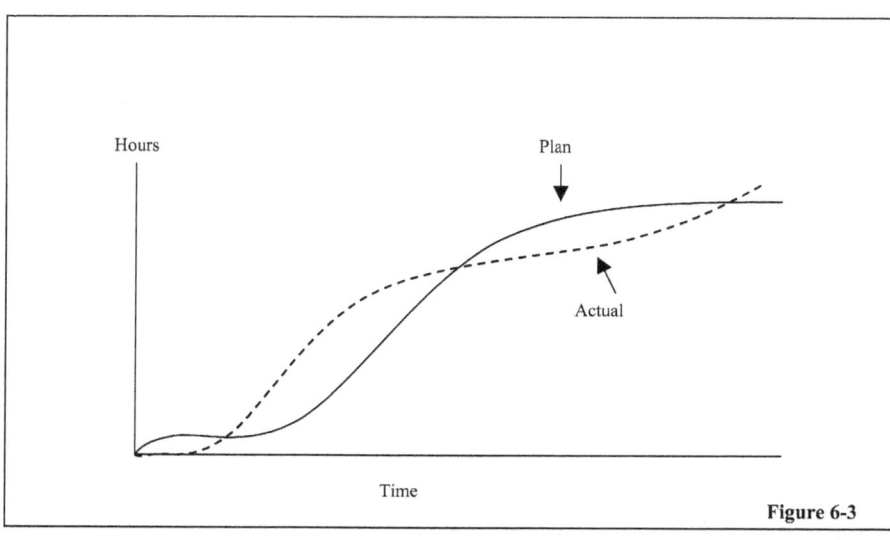

Figure 6-3

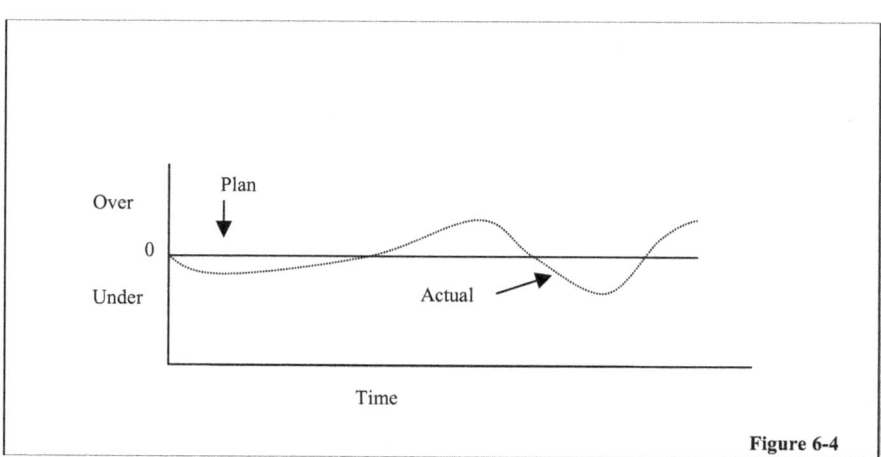

Figure 6-4

Earned Value Parameters: The EVM system depends on the tracking of three measurements of the project.

1. Budgeted Cost of Work Schedule (BCWS). When we establish the three project baselines we definitively set the cost and schedule baselines. Each of the activities in the project has its own estimated cost and schedule. The BCWS is the cumulative budget plotted on a time axis that shows when the expenditure is supposed to be made according to the project plan. Please note that according to the *Guide to the PMBOK*, this term has been replaced with the term planned value. However, they both are being used today.

2. Actual Cost of Work Performed (ACWP). As the project progresses, actual cost is accumulated. This cumulative actual cost is plotted along the same time axis. The actual cost is plotted for every reporting time period.

3. Budgeted Cost of Work Performed (BCWP). This value is also called earned value. This is the cumulative plot of the value of the work actually completed. The value of the work is equal to the budget that was estimated for the work. The cumulative budgeted cost of work performed is plotted on the same time axis. The earned value is plotted for every time period based on the actual work that is accomplished.

If the project follows the project plan, each of these three parameters are exactly the same. Significant deviations between the values of the three parameters are cause for concern (Figure 6-5).

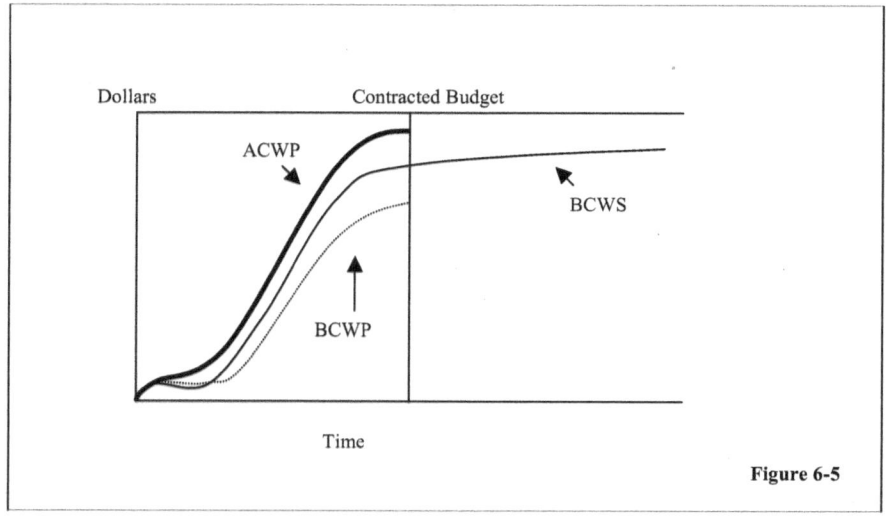

Figure 6-5

Difficulties in Data Collection: Plotting the BCWS is rather straightforward. Care must be taken that the timing and amounts that are plotted as BCWS are the same and that the timing is the same as when they are reported as actual expenditures.

In the area of material cost, the timing of the budget and the reporting of the actual expenditure are important. Expenditure may be recognized when the commitment is made to purchase the material, when the material is delivered, when the material is accepted, when it is invoiced, or when it is paid for. All of these dates must be quite different points in time. Care must be taken so that the timing of the BCWS matched the timing of the ACWP.

In the area of labor cost, difficulties frequently arise in the development of these estimates as well. Companies frequently do not like to have their estimators know the salary cost of individual employees. People are generally grouped together by similar skills. Within the group there can be a wide range of salaries. Since it is usually not possible to determine exactly who will be working on a project when the work is actually done, the average cost of a person in the group is still used.

It may seem that this is the right thing to do, but look at the effect on the project manager. The project manager is going to be charged the same amount per hour regardless of which person in the group is used to do the work. The project manager will naturally try to get the best person of the highest skill and experience regardless of who the project really needs. This situation creates more demand for the more senior people, while the junior people are underutilized.

A better situation would be to budget to the average cost for a person in the skill group and then collect the actual cost according to the person's actual salary. This would allow the project manager to select the less skilled person if possible and trade time and rework for lower salary cost.

Reporting Work Complete: Frequently there is a difficulty in reporting work completed on the project. Many people tend to report that the percent that is complete on an activity is the same as the percent of the time than has elapsed. Thus, if 50 percent of the time to do an activity in the project has passed but only 25 percent of the work is actually done, misleading reposts could result.

There are several approaches to solving this problem. The "50-50 rule" is one such approach. In this approach to earned value data collection, 50 percent of the earned value is credited as earned value when the activity is begun. The remaining 50 percent is not credited until all of the work is completed.

The 50-50 rule encourages the project team to begin working on activities in the project, since they get 50 percent of the earned value for just starting an activity. As time goes by, the actual cost of work performed accumulates, and the project team is motivated to complete the work on the activity so that the additional 50 percent of the earned value can be credited. This creates an incentive to start work and another incentive to finish work that has been started. This solves the problem of reporting percent complete, and there should be few arguments about whether work is actually begun or is complete on a project activity.

There are many variations of the 50-50 rule. Popular uses include the 20-80 rule and the 0-100 rule. These allow differing percentages of the earned value of the work to be claimed at the start and completion of the work.

Examples: In Figure 6-6, the BCWP is higher than BCWS. This means that the project is ahead of schedule. More activities have been completed than were planned to be completed at this time. This can be good. The ACWP is higher than the BCWS as well. It is also higher than the BCWP. This means that we are spending more money to accomplish work than the BCWP for that work.

This could mean that the manager of this part of the project is working people overtime in anticipation of a problem that may come to pass in the near future. There could be many explanations for these irregularities. The report tells us that we should investigate to find out the cause for this.

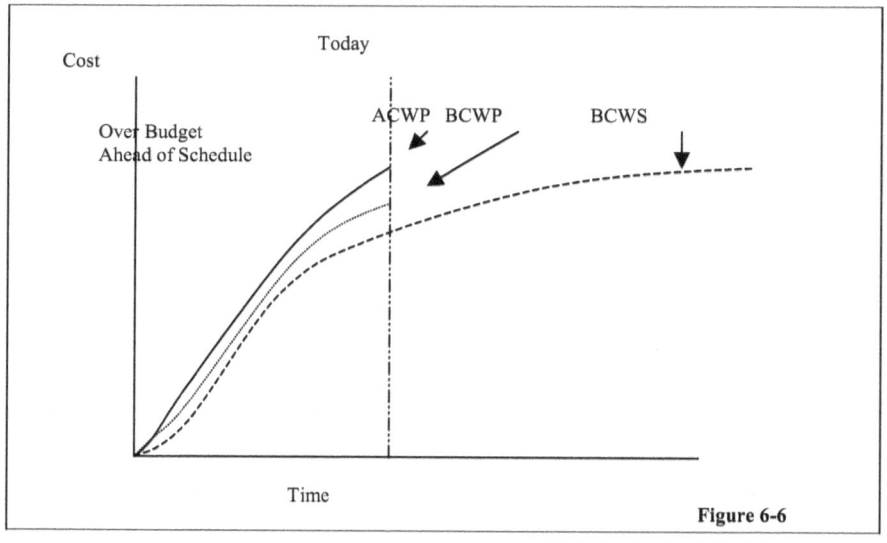

Figure 6-6

In Figure 6-7, the BCWP is above the BCWS. Again this means that the project is ahead of schedule. More activities are being completed and their Earned Value is being credited faster than planned. The ACWP is lower than the BCWP. This means that we are spending less money than the Earned Value of the work that is being completed.

While this looks like a good situation, ahead of schedule and under budget, it is still not following the project plan. It is possible that things are just going well. It is also possible that some if the work is not being done as planned and that the quality of the work performed is suffering.

In Figure 6-8, the BCWP is less than the BCWS. This means that the project is behind schedule. The ACWP is less than the BCWP. This means that work is being accomplished with less cost than planned. A possible explanation for this situation is that the project is understaffed, but the people working on the tasks that are being done are doing a better-than-average job.

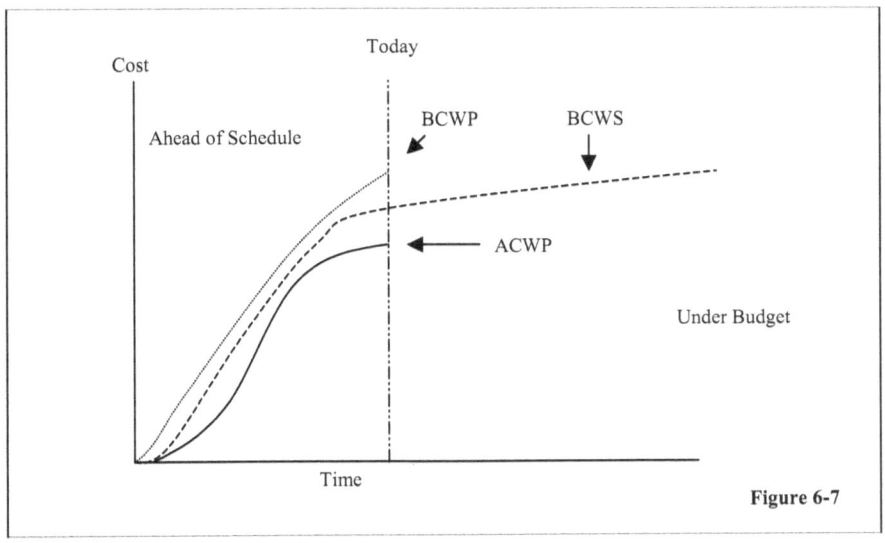

Figure 6-7

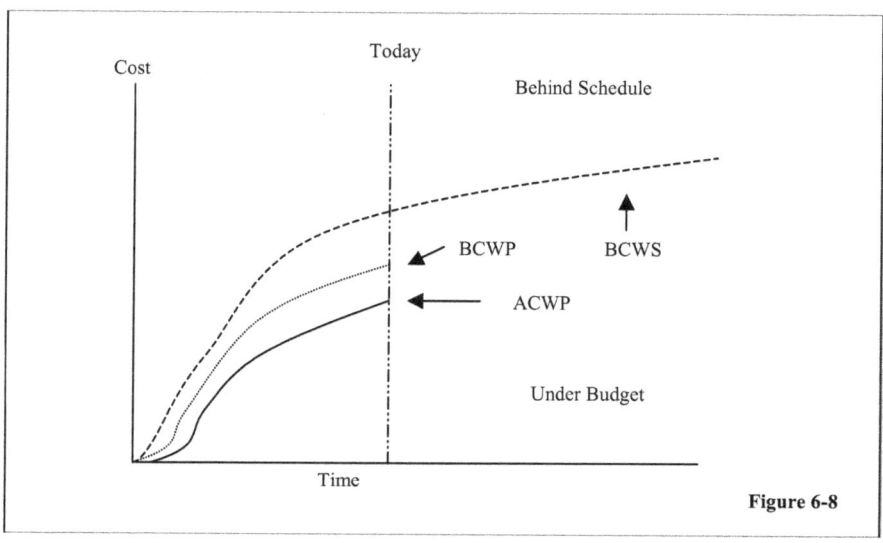

Figure 6-8

Calculated Values for Earned Value Reports:

- Budget At Completion (BAT). The BAC is a point representing the total budget if the project. On a cumulative plot it will be the last point on the BCWS curve. The BCWS cannot be greater than the BAC

- Cost Variance (CV). This is the difference between the work that is actually completed and the cost expended to accomplish the work. A positive variance is good, and a negative is bad.

$$CV = BCWP—ACWP$$

- Schedule Variance (SV). This is the difference between the work that is actually completed and the work that was expected to be completed at this time. A positive variance is good, and a negative variance is bad.

$$SV = BCWP—BCWS$$

- Cost Performance Index (CPI).

$$CPI = BCWP \div ACWP$$

- Schedule Performance Index (SPI).

$$SPI = BCWP \div BCWS$$

- Indexes. Indexes are used when consistent numbers are required. Cost and schedule variance is measured in dollars. In a larger project, say $100 million, a $100,000 cost or schedule variance might not be too significant, but in a small project, say $300,000, a $100,000 cost of schedule variance might be significant.

Cost and schedule variances also vary depending on what phase the project is in. Early in the project small variances may be significant, and later in the project these same size variances may not be terribly significant. For this reason we use indexes.

Cost Performance Index is the BCWP divided by the ACWP. This is the amount of work accomplished per dollar of actual cost spent.

The Schedule Performance Index is the BCWP divided by the BCWS. This is the amount of work accomplished per dollar of budgeted cost expected to be spent.

- Estimate AT Completion (EAC).

$$EAC = BAC \div CPI$$

The EAC is an estimate of the project cost at the completion of the project. This is the BAC adjusted for current performance to date. It says that if the project continues along at its present level of performance to cost, the EAC will be the final project cost. This is a pessimistic value, since it says that the mistakes that have been made in the project are expected to continue for the remainder of the project.

This is the way most often used for calculating the EAC. There are several other forms of the EAC that can be used that yield different results. One form that can be seen for the EAC is identical to the one presented earlier.

$$EAC = ACWP + (Remaining\ BCWS \div CPI)$$

Since the remaining BCWS in the project is simply the difference between the total work that has been completed to date, the BCWP, thus:

$$\text{Remaining BCWS} = \text{BAC} - \text{BCWP}$$

And the ACWP could be stated as:

$$\text{ACWP} = \text{BCWP} \div \text{CPI}$$

Substituting, we get the following:

$$\text{EAC} = (\text{BCWP} \div \text{CPI}) + ([\text{BAC} - \text{BCWP}] \div \text{CPI})$$
$$\text{EAC} = (\text{BCWP} - \text{BCWP} + \text{BAC}) \div \text{CPI}$$
$$\text{EAC} = \text{BAC} \div \text{CPI}$$

A more optimistic approach would be to assume that the mistakes on the project that have occurred so far are not going to continue and the project from now on will go according to plan. It is the sum of the ACWP, which is what has been spent to date and cannot be improved, plus the amount of work remaining to be done.

$$\text{EAC} = \text{ACWP} + \text{Remaining BCWS}$$
$$\text{EAC} = \text{ACWP} + \text{BAC} - \text{BCWP}$$

Of course, the most optimistic view is that the project will not only improve its performance from now until the end of the project but that the expenditures over budget to date will be recovered by the end of the project. This is a mistake often made by project managers. Generally, if a project is over budget when 25 percent of the project is complete, the project will be completed with an over budget condition greater than 25 percent and not less than 25 percent.

- Estimate To Complete (ETC). The ETC is the remaining budget required to complete the project if work continues at the present performance rate.

$$\text{ETC} = \text{EAC} - \text{ACWP}$$

There are many other calculations used in the earned value management (EVM) reporting system, but these are the calculations that are accepted by most people throughout the world (Figure 6-9)

Week	BCWS	ACWP	BCWP	CV	SV	CPI	SPI	EAC	ETC
1	1,000	1,000	1,000	0	0	1.00	1.00	16,000.00	15,000.00
2	2,000	2,000	2,000	0	0	1.00	1.00	16,000.00	14,000.00
3	4,000	5,000	4,000	-1,000	0	0.80	1.00	20,000.00	15,000.00
4	7,000	8,000	6,000	-2,000	-1,000	0.75	0.86	21,333.33	13,333.33
5	10,000	12,000	9,000	-3,000	-1,000	0.75	0.90	21,333.33	9,333.33
6	12,000	13,000	11,000	-2,000	-1,000	0.85	0.92	18,909.09	5,909.09
7	13,000	14,000	11,500	-2,500	-1,500	0.82	0.88	19,478.26	5,478.26
8	14,000	14,500	13,000	-1,500	-1,000	0.90	0.93	17,846.15	3,346.15
9	15,000	15,000	14,500	-500	-500	0.97	0.97	16,551.72	1,551.72
10	16,000	16,000	15,500	-500	-500	0.97	0.97	16,516.13	516.13
11	16,000	17,000	16,000	-1,000	0	0.94	1.00	17,000.00	0.00
BAC	16,000								

Figure 6-9

Financial Measures: The business risks of a project can be best understood by looking at some of the financial measurements that are commonly applied to business decisions. It is important to recognize that many of the costs associated with a project do not stop once the project has been delivered and each of the stakeholders has accepted the project.

The simplest way to think of project desirability is to consider the benefit cost ratio: all of the benefits of doing something divided by all of the costs to accomplish it. Any sort of business consideration can be evaluated with this simple measure. If the benefit cost ratio is 1.0 or greater, it is good, and if it is less than one, it is not good.

Life cycle costing is the cost and benefits of a project that begin when the first effort is made on behalf of the project and continue through the conceptual phase, the planning phase, the execution phase, the closeout phase, the warranty period, and on until the project is disposed of. When projects are delivered to the customer there are many costs that will continue through the life of the project. Maintenance, service, additions, and modifications are items that will continue after delivery. Some of these will result in additional cost, such as warranty repairs, and others will result in additional benefits, such as additions and modifications.

Sunk cost is a term used to indicate the amount of money that has already been spent on a project. This is money that we no longer have any control over. Although it seems that if a project is currently very much over budget it would make sense to complete the project and collect the benefits, most financial managers hold that sunk costs should not be considered in making decisions as to whether to continue a project or not.

For example, a $300,000 project is 50 percent complete but is over budget by 30 percent. Revenue from the project is estimated to be $350,000. Based on this information it is estimated that the project, when complete, will cost $400,000. Should the project continue? IF the project stops today, $200,000 in sunk cost, and no revenue made. If the project is completed, a loss of $50,000 will occur. From this point of view of many managers, all other things being equal, it is better to stop the project and invest the remaining $250,000 that it would take to complete the project in another project that is more profitable. Of course, customer commitments and future revenue based on the completion of this project may influence this decision.

Financial measures are rooted in the accounting and finance worlds. The first things that must be understood are the fundamental reports in accounting. The income statement and the balance sheet are of particular interest to the project manager, since the project manager's decisions directly influence these reports. The current trend in project management is to make project managers more responsible for the revenue cost and expenses of the project. These are the basic reports of accounting for any business. In these statements, the words *profit* and *income* are frequently interchanged. The reason that project managers must be aware of these financial measures is that if the financial measures applied to the project are favorable and the company can keep its entire project favorable, then the company's financial measures will also be favorable. The fundamental accounting equation is:

Assets = Liabilities + Owners equity

Assets are the things that a company owns, like cash, buildings, materials, etc. The liabilities are what a company owes, such as unpaid bills, long and short term debt, etc. The company owner's equity is the value of assets after the liabilities have been subtracted. In the successful operation of a company, the company takes on liabilities in order to produce goods and services that are then sold. When the goods and services are sold, there is (hopefully) a positive difference in revenue generated versus costs and expenses incurred to allow the goods and services to be sold. At the end of a project the assets that are increased should be greater than the liabilities incurred. To balance the accounting equation, this difference increases the owner's equity.

The income statement, as shown on Figure 6-10, shows where the cash flowing into and out of the company came from, and the net profit after taxes is the sum of all the money flowing into the company and all of the money flowing out of the company.

The balance sheet (Figure 6-11) is the statement that shows a breakdown of the items in the fundamental accounting equation. The assets must balance the liabilities and owner's equity.

Beyond having the income statement and the balance sheet, there are typical measures that are used to measure the health of a company. Project managers have an influence on these numbers on the company's report. But the company's reports are just the summation of the different projects and other activities of the company. It is sensible, therefore, to consider these financial measures as they apply to the individual projects as well. If all projects being done by the company are individually profitable, then the company itself must be profitable. These measures are frequently called financial ratios.

```
                Gross Sales
                Less cost of goods sold
     = Gross profit
                Less operating expenses
                        Salaries and commissions
                        Rent expenses
                        Depreciation
                        Selling expenses
                        Other operating expenses
     = Net operating income
                Plus other income
                        Interest revenue
                Less other expenses
                        Interest expenses
     = Net income before taxes
                Less income tax
     = Net income after taxes
```

Figure 6-10

```
Assets:
        Current assets
                Cash
                Accounts receivable
                Inventory
                Prepaid expenses
        Fixed assets
                Plants and equipment
                Furniture and fixtures
                Less accumulated depreciation
                Total assets
Liabilities:
        Current liabilities
                Accounts payable
                Unpaid salaries
        Long term liabilities
                Long term debt
Owner's equity:
        Common stock
        Preferred stock
        Retained earnings
        Total liabilities
Total assets = Total liabilities
```

Figure 6-11

7

COMMUNICATIONS MANAGEMENT

Communications Planning
Information Distribution
Performance Reporting
Management by Walking Around

Communications Planning

Probably the single most important thing in project management is communications. It is said that if good communications exist in a project, the team will be motivated, and the project will succeed in spite of problems that might kill another project. It is essential that project managers have a good understanding of communications.

It is generally agreed among project managers that communications skills are the most important skills that a project manager can have. These skills are considered to be more important than organizational skills, team building skills, and leadership skills, and they are certainly considered more important for project managers than technical skills (Figure 7-1). It is often said that if a project manager has good communications skills and no other skills at all, the project team will get the project completed successfully in spite of the project manager.

According to the *Guide to the PMBOK*, communications management in projects is the process required to ensure timely and appropriate generation, collection, dissemination, storage, and ultimately disposition of project information.

Which of the following do you consider important project management skills?	
Communication Skills	84%
Organization Skills	75%
Team Building Skills	72%
Leadership Skills	68%
Technological Skills	48%

Figure 7-1

Communicating is the process of delivering a message to another with understanding. We should first review the terms to make sure we are communicating properly.

Thinking: The sender frames the ideas and creates the message that he or she wants to send.

Encoding: The encoding process consists of formatting the message into some transmittable form. This makes the communication possible. The language, written and spoken words, facial expressions, body language, and other means of transmitting an idea can be used. Some times communication we do not wish to send is sent anyway. We can communicate by physically touching someone. We can communicate by making some sort of a physical gesture such as pointing finger.

Symbols: All sorts of symbols can be used to communicate. Symbols stand in the place of something we have experienced initially. A picture of a person is a symbol of that person. Words are symbols for the objects or ideas they represent.

Transmitting: This is the process of moving the message from the sender to the receiver. The medium used might be air waves, as in the use of spoken words; electronically, as in email, telephone, and fax; visual signals, or combinations of these.

Perceiving: The receiver must have recognition that the message is coming. If there is no perception of the message then the message is never received. Ultimately the message must enter the receiver by means of one of a person's five senses: sight, sound, smell, taste, or touch.

Decoding: The receiver must now take the message and convert it into some form that can be understood.

Understanding: If there is no understanding, there is no message. The message must have some understandable meaning for the receiver.

Information Distribution

Barriers to Communications

There can be many barriers to communication. Messages can be blocked or distorted, and as a result, their meaning can be changes considerably.

Distributed Sources: The source of a communication may be wrong about what he or she is communicating. It can be that the source is really wrong, or it may be that we are just convinced that the source is wrong. When this condition exists in an extreme way, it makes no difference what is really said. The perception of the message will be similar to what is expected.

Distorted Perceptions: Many times the receiver is not in the proper frame of mind to receive the message. This may be due to many factors, such as the environment, the mood of the receiver, or the subject matter being delivered. The status of the person sending the message may have an effect as well. When something is being said by the person working in the next room, the effectiveness of the communication will be different than if the CEO of the company. So we can say that motivation and needs and even his or her experience affect a person's perception.

The receiver's perception is also affected by the need to connect the new message to already received information that is stored in his or her memory. We try to connect new information to the old information in order to make it meaningful.

Transmission Errors: There are a number of reasons why a message is not properly received, and language is one of the most common problems. Not only are the different words of different languages a problem, but the cultural difference between people who speak different languages results in errors in communication even if the meaning is the same.

Receiving and sending messages can only be done within the framework of common experience and understanding. When the experience and understanding are different, communication is difficult.

When you deal with people from different cultural backgrounds, care must be taken with the choice of words that you use. There are significant cultural differences among people from different parts of the same country and even among people from different neighborhoods within the same city.

Improving Communications Skills

I have been raised in three different cultures (countries). I have also been in many countries as visitor or conducted business in Europe, Asia, as well as United States. Thus, I can say that I have a very diverse background when it comes to dealing with people from different parts of world.

Based on my experience, I came up with the following guidelines that will help improving your communications.

Reduce the Message to its Simplest Terms: When you communicate with someone, keep the message as simple as possible. Many times the message is complicated with unnecessary details about the rationale and the justification of a project when the listener is already convinced and just wants to know what to do.

Make the Message Relevant for the Receiver: Good communications come when the receiver is interested and has something at stake in the message. If the message is relevant, then the receiver is more likely to get a more complete meaning. We have all been in the situation where someone is telling us about something that is not relevant to us. Our attention wanders off to some other area, and we actually do not hear anything that is said for a period of time.

Organize the Message into a Series of Stages: One of the reasons that verbal communication succeeds over written communication is the opportunity to keep things simple. The sender can send a simple part of the message and receive feedback on that too. In this way the message is kept simple, and the receiver is brought to the complete understanding of the full message, one piece at a time. You may have heard this question, "How do you eat an elephant?" The answer is, "One bite at a time!" But if it takes too long, the elephant may spoil, and the message may be lost.

Repeat the Key Point: Because listening takes place a very small percentage of the time, it is important to repeat the important points of the message. As communication takes place, it is a good idea to go back a few steps and summarize what has gone before. This allows repetition of some of the major points and ensures that the receiver is getting all of the important points in the message.

Improving Listening Skills

Many times when we listen we do not hear what is being said to us. It is only possible to concentrate on what is being said for a small portion of the time. There are several things to remember: don't interrupt, put the speaker at ease, appear interested, cut out distractions, and periodically sum up what was said.

Don't Interrupt: One of the most disruptive things that can be done while someone is trying to communicate a message is to interrupt him or her. This stops the speaker's chain of thought and makes him or her feel that you are not interested in what the speaker has to say. The offended feeling on the part of the sender of the message may be enough to make the person angry if it is done repeatedly. Eventually this will reduce the effectiveness of the communication. There are times when this is used as a tactic. If a meeting is going in a direction that you do not like, sometimes by repeatedly interrupting you can get the speaker so upset that the meeting can be postponed, giving you enough time to gather more information to make the meeting go along a different course. However, this is not recommended.

Put the Speaker at Ease: Many times that speaker in a meeting is nervous and uncomfortable in the speaking role. To encourage the speaker you can make comments before and during the meeting to make it known that you are looking forward to what the speaker has to say and what an important contribution the speaker will be making to the meeting. During the presentation, nod your head in agreement and smile at some of the speaker's comments if possible. All of this creates a feeling of confidence and trust in the speaker.

It is important that projects managers have good presentation skills. Project managers are frequently called upon to make formal and informal presentations to other managers, clients, stakeholders, and the like. Project managers must be able to convey the information in a way that is comprehensible to their audience.

Appear Interested: Crating the impression that you are very interested in what is being said will do a lot to make the speaker feel at ease with the audience and will also make you retain more of the information that is being sent by the speaker.

Cut Out Distractions: Listening can be improved greatly by improving the environment where the communication is taking place. Noisy distracting places severely inhibit communications, while quiet places with no telephones and a closed door will greatly improve them. Asking all of the attendees to turn off cellular phones and pagers or at least put them on their vibrating mode will help to improve the environment.

Periodically Sum Up What Was Said: Listening can be further improved by stopping periodically in the meeting and summarizing what has been said. By doing this you are essentially repeating what was said in a different way. All of the attendees in the meeting will hear again what was said but in a different way, and their retention will be higher. Summing up also has the side benefit of making the speaker relax and the message that the speaker delivers will be more accurate and presented better.

Verbal and Written Communications

Many people think that there is no better way to communicate than through written messages and that verbal communications should be used sparingly. Today, with the use of email this feeling is becoming stronger. It is not unusual to see email messages being exchanged between people sitting ten feet from one another. Verbal and written communications each has its place, and it is important that the correct medium be used for the correct communication.

Verbal communications are faster than written ones; they allow us to keep the message simple and present one thought at a time to the listener. Verbal communications are two way, so we are able to get feedback from the receiver before going on. If the feedback coming from the receiver does not confirm that he or she got the message, the message can be modified and the point made in another way. Questions can be raised by the receiver to help clarify the point.

Written communications can be more detailed than verbal ones and can be used to explain something that is quite complex and requires more explanation than the receiver can absorb in a short verbal exchange. The written communication can be more organized than verbal communication, and if it is properly organized, the receiver is able to go back and review material already read.

One of the reasons why so many people use email is the timing issue. Email can be sent quickly when the sender has the time and motivation to send it. It is read and acted upon when the receiver has the time and motivation to act on it. In many ways this is much better than communicating by telephone. While the telephone gives instant communication, the person being called is usually interrupted while doing something and must change his or her thinking to deal with the person calling on the telephone.

Formal and Informal Communications

Formal Communications: Project managers and members of their project team are frequently required to make formal presentations to their managers, their customers, and various other stakeholders in the project. In order to accomplish this it is necessary for them to have good presentation skills.

Today we are fortunate that there is much in the way of computer software for presentations that makes this formerly expensive chore easy and inexpensive to accomplish. One of the most popular software packages is Microsoft PowerPoint. This software makes formal presentations easy. Digital photography is now widely available, so that photographs can be easily inserted into the presentation to make it more meaningful. Video projection is also widely available, so that the tedious process of making presentation graphics on transparencies is no longer necessary.

Distance conferencing is now widely used. Video and audio connections between conference rooms eliminate the need to have people travel to distant locations to attend meetings. This not only reduces the cost of travel but significantly saves time that could be devoted to more direct project work.

The internet has proven to be a great communication tool for project management. Project data from various parts of a project located in remote parts of the world can be easily shared and combined with other projects data through the internet.

Email has already changed the way we communicate. For most of us, the use of email changed the way we do business. Unlike telephone calls, which are almost always an interruption in what we are doing, the email we receive is looked at when we want to. This allows us to pay close attention to what is being communicated and carefully respond to inquiries.

Informal Communications: Here is an example how communications are handled in the military. One of the problems in any military organization is the structure of the military chain of command. The strict chain of command is required because, when fighting a war, it is critical that legitimate orders be carried out quickly. There is usually no time for discussion, and the commanders do not usually have the time to explain things to the subordinates who are to carry out the orders. It is important that each subordinate communicates to his or her superior officer and not deviate from that order. It would lead to confusion if an officer would go directly to a subordinate three levels below the officer.

The problem is that the military are not always engaged in war and fighting. Most of the time they are engaged in the business keeping the forces ready to fight. This part of the military function is more like an everyday business. As we have seen, in a company, having free and open communications is better than having a strict chain of command. It is not possible to have an organization work two different ways.

The problem is solved by having parties. For example, the U.S. Navy has frequent cocktail parties. When you attend these types of parties you will observe that there are only a few people sitting. This is because the party allows people to circulate regardless of rank and order in the chain of command. If one person needs to get information from another, he or she could do it this way without going through the formality of the chain of command.

Often in project management there is a need for formal communications. The normal methods of communication between the project team and the stakeholders should be open and free, but there are times when formal communications are necessary. When major milestones in the project are being passed and agreement must be received from all stakeholders, formal communications are necessary. When authorized project changes are made, it is necessary to have formal communications. As the number of persons involved in a decision is increased, the need for formal communications increases as well.

Performance Review and Reporting

One of the problems with matrix management is the problem of ensuring that all employees and members of the project team have good and fair performance reviews.

In the early days of matrix management one of the major difficulties was performance reviews. A person typically would come to work on a project, work on it for a period of time, and then move back to his or her functional department or to another project. The project manager concentrated on the project and the customer and did not take the time for performance appraisals. When the employee was assigned to the functional department, he or she experienced less stress and less urgency than when working on a project. The employee relaxed more and took vacations and sick days when working in his or her functional areas. At the end of an employee's review period, the functional manager had little to base any appraisal on except the times when the employee was working in the functional area. As a result, the employee was given a satisfactory appraisal when perhaps his or her project work had been outstanding.

A simple communication device may be used to eliminate this problem. The project manager meets with the person when he or she first joins the project. At this first meeting the project manager starts a plain sheet of paper and makes comments about the suggested assignments for the person. At the end of the meeting the project manager makes a copy of the notes to give to the individual and files the original. In two weeks another meeting is held to review the progress that has been made since the last meeting. Again notes are made and copied and given to the individual. As time goes on these notes accumulate and make up a written history of the work done on the project, successes and failures. When the employee leaves the project, the project manager makes another copy of these notes and sends them to the person's functional manager. This way the functional manager has a set of notes on the performance of the individual.

Management by Walking Around

Management by walking around is a concept that actually uses a lot of common sense. It is particularly effective for managers that are a little self-conscious about talking to people. Some of these managers are reluctant to come out of their offices and talk to their own people. Such reclusive managers don't communicate well.

It is easier to show how to do management by walking around than to explain it. The manager participating the technique of management by walking around makes a commitment to do this for a half-hour to an hour each day. This may seem like a lot of time to the manager at first, but the benefits are derived will save more time than the time spent doing this.

The manager leaves his or her office and starts walking around the project-team office-space. When a member of the project team is approached, the manager says something like, "How was your golf game this week?" (Of course, the prudent manager would know that the person he or she is talking to actually plays golf.) The manager opens up the conversation with a casual statement, and the team member begins to talk about his or her latest escapade on the golf links. Human nature demands that the team member change the subject of the conversation in a short time. He or she does not want to excessively talk about golf with the project manager. Soon the team member is discussing the project. When this happens all of the anxiety that is often present disappears, and free and honest communication takes place.

If the manager had taken a different approach to this conversation, the results might have been different. If the project manager had come to this team member and said, "Hey John, how are things going on your part of the project?" John would have first asked himself things like, "Why is the boss asking me this?" "Something is wrong and I don't even know about it." "My review is due, what can I say?" All these things and more go through a person's mind when he or she is put on the spot. This results in anxiety. The team member gives a minimal response to the manager, and poor communication is the result.

8

RISK MANAGEMENT

Risk Planning
Risk Identification
Risk Response
Budgeting for Risk
Risk Monitoring and Control

Risk Planning

Risk management is one of the most important areas of project management that must be considered. Companies that want to compete successfully have adopted project management as a method of managing their companies. They have had to learn how to define and control project scope, schedule, and cost as baselines, and they have had to learn all of the control elements necessary to make successful projects. But many of these companies have yet to learn how to manage risks involved in managing a project.

As discussed previously, one of the principles involved in good project management is establishing three baselines. The cost, schedule, and scope baselines are essential to managing a project. These three constraints on a project serve to define the project and give us the goals that are to be obtained. The cost baseline of the project must represent all of the cost that will be incurred in the project. The scope baseline must represent all of the work that has to be done in the project. The schedule baseline must represent all of the time that it is going to take to do the project.

When we discussed project scope, we emphasized the importance of discovering and documenting all of the work that has to be done in the project. The scope of the project must also include the work that must be done to handle the work that was not expected to be necessary. When this work is included in the project plan, it affects the scope and schedule baselines.

All of this work has some probability of occurring. Work that has a probability of greater than zero but less than 100 percent of occurring is considered to be a risk. Risks can have a positive or negative effect. They can produce benefits for the project, or they can produce loss for the project. The *Guide to PMBOK* defines a risk event as "a discrete occurrence that may affect the project for better or worse."

Risks can be divided into known and unknown risks. Known risks are those risks that can be identified. Unknown risks are those that cannot be identified, but we can recognize the effect of these unknown risks, and we can plan for them. This planning can be accomplished by looking at expert opinion and observations of similar projects and evaluating the risks that occurred there, and then adjusting schedules and budgets accordingly.

When to Do Risk Management
Risk management must be done during the whole life of the project. In the beginning of the conceptual stage of the project, risks are identified almost without effort as the different aspects of the project are discussed. It is important that when these risks are thought of, they are recorded and placed in a risk management file or folder so that they can be dealt with later in the project.

As time goes by and progress is made on the project, the risks need to be reviewed, and the identification process must be repeated for the discovery of new risks. This must be an ongoing, continuous process. Risks that are identified early in the project may change as time goes by. As the project advances, some risks will disappear. Other risks that were not thought of earlier will be discovered. As the possibility of the risks approaches, the risk needs to be reevaluated to be sure that the assessment of the risk made earlier is still valid.

Risk Components
The components of risk management are the factors that make up what we need to know about the risk.

Risk Identification: The identification of the risk is very important; the risk must be described in detail so that it will not be confused with any other risk or project tack that must be done. Each risk should be given an identification number. During the course of the project, as more information is gathered about the risk, all of this information can be consolidated.

Risk Probability: Since all risks have a probability of greater than zero and less than 100 percent, the probability of a risk occurring is essential to the assessment of the risk. Any risk event that has a probability of zero cannot occur and need not be considered as a risk. A risk event that has a probability of 100 percent is not a risk. It has a certainty of occurring and must be planned for in the project plan.

Risk Impact: Risk impact is the cost of the risk if it occurs. This, in its qualitative measure is the pain level of the risk. Quantitative measures include the impact of the identified risk in terms of schedule days, effort man-hours, money, etc.

Steps in Risk Management

Generally, it is thought that the risk management process is done in four steps:

1. Risk planning (*discussed above*)
2. Risk identification
3. Risk mitigation
4. Risk control and evaluation

Risk Identification: The risk identification process consists of identifying the risks and documenting them so that they will not be forgotten once they have been identified.

Risk Evaluation: The risk evaluation process consists of evaluating each risk so that the ones that will have the most severe effect on the project will receive the most attention.

Risk Mitigation: Risk mitigation consists of determining a plan to reduce, limit, or even ignore the risk and its effect on the project.

Risk Control & Evaluation: Risk control and evaluation consists of observing and reporting on the risks as time goes by. Some risks will prove to have not occurred, while others will have occurred, and the mitigation strategies will be observed to have worked or not worked.

Risk Identification

The three necessary components of risk are identification of the risk event, probability of the risk event occurring, and the impact of the risk event if it occurs. The first component we need to discuss is the identification of the risk event. In the course of identifying risk events we will call upon the project team, subject matter experts, the stakeholders, and other project managers.

There are many ways to discover and identify risks. We will discuss several of them here:

- Documentation reviews
- Brainstorming
- Delphi technique
- Normal group technique
- Crawford slip
- Expert interviews
- Checklists
- Analogy
- Diagramming Techniques

Documentation Reviews: Documentation reviews comprise reviewing all of the project materials that have been generated up to the date of this risk review. This includes reviewing lessons learned and risk management plans from previous projects, the project's work breakdown structure, and contract obligations, project baselines for scope, schedule, and budget, resource availabilities, staffing plans, suppliers, and assumptions lists.

Brainstorming: Brainstorming is probably the most popular technique of its kind. It is useful in generating any kind of list by mining the ideas of the participants. To use the technique, a meeting is called to make a comprehensive list of risks. It is important that the purpose of the meeting be explained clearly to the participants, and it is helpful if they are prepared when they arrive at the meeting. The meeting should have between ten and fifteen participants. If there are fewer than ten people, there is not enough interaction among the participants. If there are more than fifteen people, the meeting tends to be difficult to control and keep focused. The meeting should take less than two hours.

In larger projects it may be necessary to have several meetings. Each meeting deals with a separate part of the project. It is also a good idea to have a meeting to discuss the risks of the entire project.

When the meeting begins, participants can name risks that they think are important for consideration in the project. No discussion of the items listed is allowed at this time. As the participants see ideas listed, they will think of additional ideas. Each new idea will jog another from someone, and many ideas for possible risks will be listed. By seeing the other participants' ideas listed, new ideas are jogged out of memory and the list becomes quite comprehensive.

Delphi Technique: The Delphi technique is similar to brainstorming but the participants do not know one another. This technique is useful if the participants are some distance away. The Delphi technique is much more efficient and useful today than it has been in the past because of the use of email as a medium for conducting the exercise. Because the participants in this technique are anonymous, there is a tendency for one or more people to dominate the meeting. If one of the participants is a higher level manager than the others in the meeting, many of the meeting participants will be inhibited or try to show off in front of the upper level manager. All of this is avoided in the Delphi technique.

The process begins with the facilitator using a questionnaire to solicit the participants to submit risk ideas about the project. The responses by the participants are then categorized and clarified by the facilitator. The categorized, clarified list is circulated to the participants for comments or additions. The members of the group may either modify their position or not, but they must give reasons for doing so. Consensus and a detailed list of the project risks can be obtained in a few rounds.

Nominal Group Technique: In the nominal group technique, the idea is to eliminate some of the problems that occur with other techniques, particularly the problems associated with persons' inhibitions and reluctance to participate. In this technique the usual size of seven to ten persons is used. The facilitator instructs each of the participants to privately and silently list his or her ideas on a piece of a paper. When this is completed, the facilitator takes each piece of paper and lists the ideas on a flip chart or blackboard. At this time no discussion takes place.

Once all of the ideas are listed, the group discusses each idea. During the discussion, clarifications and explanations are made. Each member of the group now ranks the ideas in order of importance, again in secret. The result is a list of the risks in order of their importance. This process not only identifies risks but also does a preliminary evaluation of them.

This process reduces the effect of a high-ranking person in the group but does not eliminate it, like the Delphi technique. The nominal group technique is faster and requires less effort on the part of the facilitator than the Delphi technique.

Crawford Slip: The Crawford slip process has become popular recently. It does not require as strong a facilitator as the other techniques, and it produces a lot of ideas very quickly. A Crawford slip meeting can take place in less than half an hour.

The usual number of seven to ten participants is used, but larger groups can be accommodated, since there is a fairly small amount of interaction among the persons in the group. The facilitator begins by instructing the group that he or she will ask ten questions, one at a time. Each participant must answer each question with a different answer. The same answer cannot be used for more than one question. The participants are to write their answer to each question on a separate piece of paper. The facilitator tells the participants that they will have one minute to answer each question.

When all the participants are ready, the facilitator begins by asking question such as, "What is the most important risk to this project?" The participants write down the answer. After one minute, the facilitator repeats the same question. This is repeated ten times. The effect is that the participants are forced to think of ten separate risks in the project. Even with duplicates among the members, the number of risks identified is formidable.

Expert Interviews: Experts or, better, people with experience in this type of project or problem can be of great help in avoiding solving the same problems over and over again. Caution must be exercised whenever using expert opinions. If an expert is trusted implicitly and his or her advice is taken without question, the project can head off in the wrong direction under the influence of one so-called expert.

The use of experts, particularly those hired from outside the project organization, can be costly. Care must be taken to ensure that experts are used efficiently and effectively. Before the expert interview is conducted, the input information must be given to the expert and the goals of the interview must be clearly understood. During the interview, the information from the expert must be recorded. If more than one expert is used, the output information from the interviews should be consolidated and circulated to the other experts.

Checklists: Checklists have gained in popularity in recent years because of the ease of communications through computers and the ease of sharing information through databases. These are many commercially available databases, and many checklists are generated locally for specific companies and applications.

In their basic form, these checklists are simply predetermined lists of risks that are possible for given projects. In their specific form, they are risks that have occurred in the particular types of projects that a company has worked on in the past. Frequently, certain customers and stakeholders have particular risks associated with them that can forewarn the manager of the new project.

Analogy: From the lessons learned and the risk management plan of other projects that are similar, an analogy can be formed. By comparing two or more projects, characteristics that are similar for each project can be seen that will give insight into the risks of the new project.

Diagramming Techniques: Various types of diagramming techniques have been developed that will help in the identification of risks. Cause and effect diagrams are used to organize information and show how various items relate to one another. There are several possible risks that contribute to the main risk in question. Each of the contributing risks can be further diagrammed until there is a complete hierarchy of risks. Once diagrammed, the relationships between the risks can easily be seen.

Flow charts are diagrams that show the sequence of events that take place in a given process. They also show conditional branching. Each point on the flow diagram can be used as a possible point identifying risks.

Identification Technique	Advantages	Disadvantages
Brainstorming	▪ Encourages interaction in the group ▪ Fast ▪ Not expensive	▪ Can be dominated by an individual ▪ Can focus in specific areas only ▪ Requires strong facilitator ▪ Must control tendency of the group to evaluate
Delphi Technique	▪ Cannot be dominated by an individual ▪ Can be done remotely by email ▪ Avoids problem of early evaluation ▪ Every person must participate	▪ Time consuming ▪ Labor intensive for facilitator
Nominal Group Technique	▪ Reduces the effort of a dominant individual ▪ Allows for interaction of participants ▪ Results in a ranked list of risk ideas	▪ Time consuming ▪ Labor intensive for facilitator
Crawford Slip	▪ Fast ▪ Easy to implement ▪ Every person must participate ▪ Large number of ideas generated ▪ Able to do with larger than normal group ▪ Reduces the effect of a dominant individual	▪ Less interaction between participants
Expert Interviews	▪ Take advantage of past experience	▪ Expert may be biased ▪ Time intensive
Checklists	▪ Focused and organized ▪ Easy to use	▪ Prejudgment ▪ May not include specific items for this project
Analogy Techniques	▪ Use past experience to avoid future experiences ▪ Similar projects have many similarities	▪ Time intensive ▪ Easy to obtain data that is not relevant ▪ Analogy may be incorrect
Diagramming Techniques	▪ Clear representation of the process involved ▪ Easy to generate ▪ Many computer tools available for them	▪ Sometimes misleading ▪ Can be time consuming

Figure 8-1

Risk Response Planning

The next step in the risk management process is risk response planning. At this stage we have discovered all of the risks known to date and have assesses their impacts and probability of occurrence.

Risk response planning is the process of developing the procedures and techniques to enhance opportunities and reduce threats to the project's objectives. In this process it will be necessary to assign individuals who will be responsible for each risk and generate a response that can be used for each risk.

Risk Strategies

Risk strategies are the techniques used to reduce the effect or probability of the identified or even the unidentified risks. In terms of the risk strategy that should be employed, a qualitative or quantitative evaluation of the severity of the risk will be a guide to how much time, money, and effort should be spent on the strategy to limit the risk in question.

Avoidance

Risk avoidance means just what it says: The strategy is to avoid the risk completely. The project plan or the nature of the project is actually changed to make it impossible for the risk to occur.

Some risks, such as the risk of not having clearly defined set of user requirements, can be avoided by expending the effort to more clearly define the requirements. This may increase the time and effort previously allowed for this activity, but it will have the result of eliminating the risk.

For example, suppose our project is to design a bicycle. Let's say that during the design phase someone identified a risk of corrosion in the frame of the bicycle. If this corrosion were severe enough, it could cause a failure in the bicycle frame. This failure could cause serious injury to the person riding the bicycle at the time of failure.

The strategy exercised by the project team on this project is to redesign the components that are corrosion problems to use a corrosion resistant material such as stainless steel. This completely avoids the problem of corrosion in the bicycle frame identified risky.

The avoidance strategy cannot completely eliminate the risk. In this example, even though the bicycle is redesigned in stainless steel, if it were left outdoors by the ocean for nineteen years, it might still corrode enough to fail. However, the probability becomes so small that the risk is, for all practical purposes, eliminated.

Transfer

Transferring a risk also eliminates the risk from impacting the project. When we transfer a risk, we move the impact of the risk to some other party. When risks are transferred to another party, there is usually some sort of payment involved to induce the party to take on the risk.

Insurance is a method for transferring risk. In terms of risk management what we are doing is hiring some third party to take over the impact of the risk. In return for this, we pay a premium. For example, in 1995, the Project Management Institute (PMI) held its annual meeting in the city of New Orleans. Six months prior to this meeting, the PMI Board of Directors held their quarterly board meeting in New Orleans. The Greater New Orleans chapter hosted the board for a chapter meeting, and as the program they invited a panel of disaster and emergency management people to discuss hurricane effects on the city.

The discussion at the meeting concentrated itself with the possible results of a hurricane hitting New Orleans. The PMI board became somewhat nervous about their meeting, since it would be held in prime hurricane season. The recognized that the revenue from the annual meeting was a significant part of their operating budget, and they could not afford to take this loss.

The result of this nervousness was that PMI board purchased convention insurance for the first time. As a result they paid a premium to the insurance company to take their risk of having their meeting cancelled. The insurance company agreed to pay PMI in the event of some disaster occurring which would force the board to cancel the meeting. To show that this was indeed a real risk, three years later, a similar meeting was held by the Petroleum Engineers Association; the meeting was cancelled due to a hurricane.

Contracting

Another way of transferring risk is to contract the risk to an outside vendor. If this is done with a firm fixed-price contract, the risk is effectively transferred to the vendor. Generally, in firm fixed-price contracts, the vendor always raises the price of the service to compensate for the effect of the risk. Warrantees, performance bonds, and guarantees are additional methods for transferring risk.

Acceptance

The acceptance of risk means that the project team has decided not to change the project in any way to compensate for the risk. The risk will be dealt with if it occurs.

Passive acceptance is doing nothing at all about the risk. If the risk actually occurs, the project team will develop a way to work around the risk or to correct its effects.

Active acceptance is developing a plan of action to be taken in anticipation of the risk coming. This action will result in a contingency plan. The contingency plan can be implemented if triggers occur, indicating the possibility of the risk occurring. In addition to the contingency plan, a fallback plan may be created as well. A fallback plan is an additional contingency plan to use in the event that the first contingency plan fails.

Mitigation

The strategies that we have discussed, have gotten rid of the risk entirely, transferred it to someone else, or just taken acceptance to the risk, either passively or actively. Risk mitigation is an effort to reduce the probability or impact of the risk to a point where the risk can be accepted. Adding additional tests, hiring duplicate suppliers, adding more expert personnel, designing prototypes, or other ways of changing the conditions under which the risk can occur are ways of mitigation risk.

The important difference in risk mitigation is that it reduces the risk to a level where we can accept it and its consequences. Adding specific work to the project plan employs the mitigation strategy. This work will always be done regardless of whether the risk occurs. The mitigation tasks are specific project tasks that are added to the project plan to reduce the impact or probability of the risk.

It should be clear that an overall risk strategy should be designed to deal with risks by accepting them as they are, avoiding them by eliminating them from being possible, transferring them to another's responsibility, or reducing their impacts and/or probability to an acceptable level.

Risk Opportunities

Risks that are opportunities should be treated in a different way from risks that are damaging to the project. Generally, the same strategies should be used, with the exception that risks are opportunities should not be deflected or transferred. This type of risk should be accepted or encouraged, a sort of mitigation in reverse.

Budgeting for Risk

In keeping with the principle that project baselines are the definite commitment for the project, the project budget and schedules should be those that the project is truly expected to meet. That is, the budget is the budget that is really expected to be spent when the project is complete, and the schedule should allow for sufficient time to do the project. This budget and schedule must include the time for managing and overcoming risks. In Chapter 5, Time Management, we looked at dealing with schedule contingency. Here we will discuss planning for budget contingency.

Funds that are to be used for mitigation, avoidance, or transfer are budgeted in with the rest of the committed project work. These are actual tasks that must be done, or they are funds that will be spent regardless of whether or not the risk occurs. But how do we budget for the work that must be done only if the risk occurs?

There are two kinds of risks that must be dealt with, known risks and unknown risks. Known risks are the risks that were identified in the identification process of risk management, as discussed earlier. Unknown risks are the ones that we know will probably occur on this project, because unknown and unexpected risks have occurred before on projects of this type.

Known risks should be handled by the creation of a contingency budget. This money is not assigned to specific project tasks and is set aside and available to fund the work that must be done if and when a risk occurs. This budget should require the approval of the project manager as a means of making certain that the money is truly allocated to solve risk problems. If this money is made available too early, it will be spent early in the project on problems that occur that might have been solved within the normal course of completing the task.

Unknown risks must be funded as well. These risks are those that were not identified in the risk identification process. An estimate based on past experience with similar projects can be made. This estimate is used to create a management reserve. The management reserve is similar to the contingency budget in that it is made available to fund unknown risks when they occur. In order to prevent the inappropriate use of this budget, a person at a level above the project manager level must approve the use of these funds.

Risk Monitoring and Control

Risk monitoring and control is the process of keeping track of all the identified risks and identifying new risks as their presence becomes known and residual risks that occur when the risk management plans are implemented on individual risks. The effectiveness of the risk management plan is evaluated on an ongoing basis throughout the project.

When a risk is apparently going to take place, the contingency plan is brought into place. If there is no contingency plan, then the risk is worked on an ad hoc basis using what is termed a workaround. A workaround is an unplanned response to a negative risk event.

The concern of the project manager and the project team is that the risk response have been brought to bear on the risk as planned, that the risk response has been effective. Additional risks may develop, and additional responses may be necessary.

Risk management is a continuous process that takes place during the entire project from the beginning to end. As the project progresses, the risks that have been identified are monitored and reassessed as the time that they can take place approaches. Early warning indicators are monitored to reassess the probability and impact of the risk. As the risk approaches, the risk strategies are reviewed for appropriateness, and additional responses are planned.

As each risk occurs and is dealt with, or is avoided, these changes must be documented. Good documentation ensures that risks of this type will be dealt with in a more effective way than before and that the next project manager will benefit from "lessons learned".

9

PROCUREMENT AND CONTRACT MANAGEMENT

Procurement Management
Source Selection
Contract Administration and Management

Procurement Management

Procurement is the act of acquiring goods and services from outside the organization. The procurement process includes planning for the procurement, soliciting the sources for the desired product or services, and defining the requirements, source selection, administration, and closeout. In a free market economy the competitiveness of the product or service that is sought will have a great deal to do with the type of contract that can be written between the two parties.

Commodities

Items that are sought that are widely available and for all intents and purposes identical are considered to be commodities. In the sale of commodities there are many people offering the same product. In all cases the products are identical for the purpose for which they are intended. Familiar examples of commodities are corn, wheat, and soybeans, but electrical components that are made by a number of different firms and are relatively standardized are also commodities.

Since there are many suppliers of the same commodity, competition drives the price to the lowest level. A seller will not be able to sell a commodity if there is someone else offering the same thing for a lower price.

According to the theory of supply and demand, the price of a product rises as the demand increases. The higher price for the commodity causes other producers to enter the market until the supply increases to meet the additional demand. As demand for a commodity decreases the price that people are willing to pay for the commodity decreases. Producers of the commodity leave the market, and the supply is reduced to a level that meets the demand. Eventually, in a completely competitive environment, supply and demand will reach equilibrium.

In a contract for commodity items, the details of the contract and the description of the item being contracted for are relatively standardized.

Most of the people in the business of selling commodity items will standardize on the purchase process. With standardization it becomes easier to purchase an item from competing vendors and know that the item will be the same from each vendor.

Unique Products and Services

When we deal with unique products and services there will be some risk involved on the part of the buyer and seller that will modify the truly competitive environment. Unlike commodity buying and selling the uniqueness of a project will make it impossible to compare the offering of competitors, and many criteria other than price must be used.

Projects themselves are frequently this type of purchased item. It is necessary to evaluate many different criteria among the offerings that are made. There will be differences in quality, performance, timeliness, and cost for similar projects from different suppliers.

Perfect competition, as in the commodities type of purchasing, naturally drives the price to the lowest level that allows the producers to make an acceptable profit. In an effort to make a higher profit many companies try to add features to their product that make it unique. Once uniqueness has been established it is possible to price the unique item higher than it would be in a competitive commodity situation.

Forward Buying

Forward buying is the process of buying items in anticipation of their need. As with all things it is important to consider the cost and benefits that can result in doing this.

The advantage of forward buying is that there is some protection against running out of an item. In the world of production control this is called a "stock out". Frequently, the vendor will also give a discount for buying larger quantities. The shipping cost will usually be lower to ship a large number of items in one shipment rather than making several small shipments. This serves to reduce the cost of the product being made.

On the negative side of forward buying there is the risk that the large number of parts will become obsolete before they are used. Consider the company that purchased a large quantity of buggy whips right before the invention of the Ford automobile. Forward buying requires that the larger inventory of parts be stored in the facility as well. In most businesses floor space is valuable and better used for working the business than for storing parts.

Blanket Orders

Blanket orders are a form of forward buying. A blanket order allows the buyer to take a quantity discount without actually taking delivery on the large quantity. In a blanket order the buyer agrees to buy all of the material needed of a certain item from one or more vendors for a specified period of time. The vendor then agrees to sell the items at a discount price based on the expected quantity needed over that period of time.

As the need for the material items occurs, requests to the vendor are filled and tracked against the blanket order. At the end of the time period, the total quantity ordered and delivered to the buyer is checked against the blanket order quantity, and a cash payment is made to the buyer if the quantity has been higher and to the seller if the quantity is lower.

This arrangement has advantages for both parties. The buyer is assured of a reliable supply of parts because he or she has made s long term commitment to the vendor. The buyer gets a quantity discount without having to stock a large inventory of parts.

The seller has the advantage of having a committed customer for the duration of the blanket order. This commitment allows the seller to plan his or her own operation with the reliability that the customer will continue to purchase these items for a period of time. With the confidence that there will be future business the seller may be able to invest in equipment and facilities to make these parts for the buyer.

Split Orders

Splitting orders is a process of dividing work between two or more vendors of an item. The purpose of splitting an order is to reduce the risk that the parts may not be delivered on time or may not be of acceptable quality. The advantage of this process is that the probability of one vendor supplying acceptable parts is increased.

Let's say, for example, we have two vendors and each has a 90 percent probability of delivering on time. We could increase the probability of at least one vendor delivering on time of we give half of the order to each vendor. This is the probability of one vendor or the other delivering. (This is the addition rule of statistics.) The probability of one or the other vendor delivering on time is the probability of one vendor delivering plus the probability of the other vendor delivering given that the first vendor failed to deliver.

The probability of one vendor delivering is 90 percent. The probability of the second vendor delivering given the first vendor failed to deliver is the probability of both the first vendor not delivering and the second vendor delivering.

Probability of A or B delivering = Probability of A delivering (90%) +
*Probability of **not** A (10%) **and** the probability of B delivering (90%)*
$$P\ (A\ or\ B) + .90 + (.90\ X\ .10) + .99$$

We can increase the probability from 90 percent to 99 percent by splitting the order between the two vendors.

Splitting the order does not come without a price. The quantity discount from either of the vendors will be reduced, since only half the quantity is being purchased from each vendor. One of the vendors may not have the same quality as the preferred vendor, and this may add rework to the process.

Source Selection

Source selection involves the receipt of bids or proposals and the application of the evaluation criteria to select a provider or vendor. Many factors aside from cost or price may need to be evaluated in the source selection decision process.

- Price may be the primary determinant for an off-the-shelf item, but the lowest proposed price may not be the lowest cost if the seller proves unable to deliver the product in a timely manner.
- Proposals are often separated into technical (approach) and commercial (price) sections with each evaluated separately.
- Multiple sources may be required for critical products.

The tools and techniques described here may be used singly or in combination. For example, a weighting system may be used to:

- Select a single source who will be asked to sign a standard contract.
- Rank order all proposals to establish a negotiating sequence.

On major procurement items, this process may be repeated. A short list of qualified sellers may be selected based on a preliminary proposal, and then a more detailed evaluation will be conducted based on a more detailed and comprehensive proposal.

Contract Management

The first thing we should have is a definition of a contract. Texts on business law define a contract as follows: A contract is an agreement between competent parties, for consideration, to accomplish some lawful purpose with the terms clearly set forth.

First of all, the contract is an "agreement". This means that the parties involved must have a meeting of the minds and decide that they will do the things set forth in the contract. By this definition no contract can be forced on someone. If any kind of forcing or coercion is done, there cannot be an enforceable contract. You cannot force someone at gunpoint to sign a contract to buy goods and expect to hold the person to the contract.

The contract must be "between competent parties". This means that the people that make the agreement must be competent to make the agreement. Persons that are impaired in any way that makes them unable to make responsible decisions or people who are not of legal age are not able to make contracts. As a matter of fact, if a minor or another incompetent party enters into a contract, the contract may be enforceable on the competent party and not on the incompetent party.

The contract must be "for consideration". This means that something must be given for something else. If there is no exchange of anything, then there is no contract. There would be no point in going to the trouble to create a contract of there is no exchange. It is important to note that the consideration does not have to be something that is valuable to everyone. The consideration could easily be something that one person values and no one else does. The consideration does not need to be tangible either. Intangible consideration can be involved in any contract.

The contract must "accomplish some lawful purpose". No contract can legally be written that would violate the law. You cannot contract with someone to steal a car for you. The contract would be void at its inception.

In discussing contract management for projects we generally are interested in the relationship between a buyer and a supplier.

Make or Buy

The decision to make or buy something must be considered. Many times it will be less expensive to purchase something from an outside source than it is to make the item inside the company.

Cost is a major consideration for this, but there are many other reasons for deciding whether to purchase or make an item. If a facility has idle capacity, it may be better to make a part in-house that is normally made by an outside vendor. The excess capacity is there to be used, and the company is paying for it whether it is used or not. In a make or buy decisions it should only be necessary to consider the variable cost in this situation. If your facility has no extra capacity, then the cost of adding the capacity must be considered as well.

When it is important that strict control be maintained in the production of an item, it may be necessary to make the item instead of purchasing it. Similarly, items that involve trade secrets and innovative products should not be contracted out of the company.

Using the flexibility of the purchasing system to stabilize the workforce is desirable. Many companies have used this strategy to help maintain consistent employment levels in their companies. A company wishing to do this subcontracts some of the work to outside companies. When the demand for its product goes down, the company decreases the amount of work that the outside contractor is doing and maintains the constant level of work in its own facility. It does not take vendors long to figure this out and adjust pricing for the product to compensate them for their own stability problems.

Deciding to purchase an item may simply be a matter of a company not having the ability to produce the item. The unique skills needed for this project may not be needed in the future. Buying equipment that will be needed only for this project may not be justifiable, and it may be less costly to buy the items in question.

Contract Life Cycle

The contract life cycle must be managed like the project life cycle. The contracting process is very similar to project management processes of initialization, planning, implementation, and closeout.

In the contracting process, we consider the steps in a little more detail (Figure 9-1). The requirement of the contracting process can be considered equivalent to the initialization of the project. The requisition, solicitation, and award processes in contracting can be considered equivalent to the planning process. The contract can be considered equivalent to the implementation process. Closeout occurs at the end of the contract.

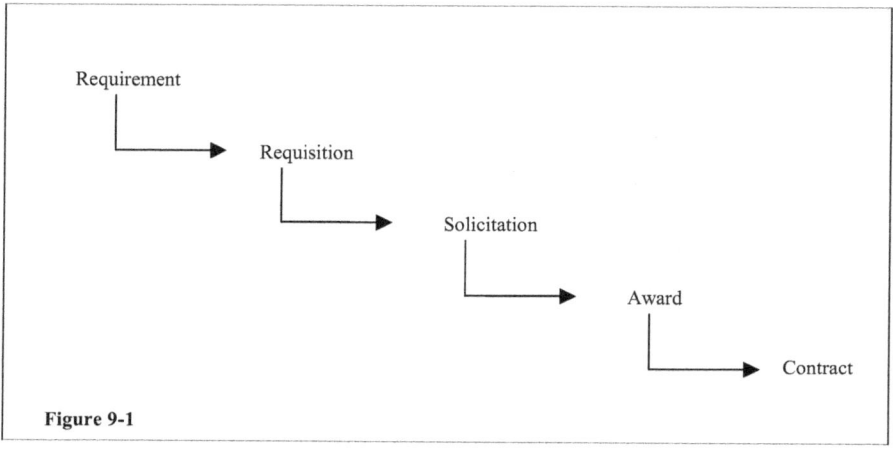

Requirement

Requisition

Solicitation

Award

Contract

Figure 9-1

Requirement Process: In the requirement process the needs of the project are identical. As in the requirements definition of the project, the requirements of the contract are identified. These requirements come from a needs assessment, and the needs are further reduced to requirements. Before the decision to purchase a good or service is made, a decision must be made as to whether the item should be purchased or made internally. Requirements are frequently stated in a document called the statement of work.

Cost estimates must be produced to help predict what the correct cost of the item should be. These cost estimates help the person doing the purchasing to determine whether or not the potential vendor is quoting a fair and agreeable price.

As in the project management requirements definition, the process begins with a determination of needs. These are items that someone wishes to have delivered. These needs are reduced by mutual agreement to requirements. The requirements are further reduced by excluding the requirements that are not justified.

Requisition Process: The requisition process consists of reviewing the specifications and statement of work and identifying qualified suppliers. During the requisition process, the requirements definition is passed to the purchasing personnel. These may or may not be part of the project team. The specifications and statement of work are reviewed, but now there is input from the purchasing function. This input provides cost information that may further reduce the requirement of items that are now demand to be impractical.

At this time all of the signatures necessary to procure the item are added to the requisition. Certain signatures are required before the company can be committed to make expenditure and other signatures are necessary to be sure that all necessary persons are informed about the purchase being made.

Solicitation Process: The solicitation process involves getting bids or proposals. During this process vendors are asked to participate in the contest of becoming the chosen vendor. In the case of commodity purchases it may only be necessary to evaluate the price of the item being supplied. In the case of unique items it may be necessary to evaluate many different aspects of the vendor and the product that is proposed.

Award Process: During the awarding process, one vendor is selected from the ones solicited. At this time the contract is written, negotiated, and signed by both parties.

The writing and signing of the contract can be simple, as in the purchase of a commodity. In the purchasing of common items the contract is generally a standard item that is written on the back of a purchase order. Many times these contracts are written in very light ink and in very small fonts.

For more complex purchases, the contract may have to be negotiated, and specific terms and conditions for this particular contract must be agreed to. The more detailed the contract, the more complex this part of the contracting cycle will be.

Contract Process: The contracting process is the final stage of the contracting cycle. In this process, the contract is actually carried out. The vendor and the purchaser must follow the planning process, organize the work staff for the work to be done, and control the contract. The purchaser and the seller must both be responsible for their part of the contract.

Contract Types

In the world of commerce nearly any kind of agreement can be made that will satisfy the needs of both parties of the contract. Whenever there is a contract, there is always business risk. The business risk is that there can be a positive or negative outcome to the contract, depending on the risks involved and whether they work out favorably or not (Figure 9-2).

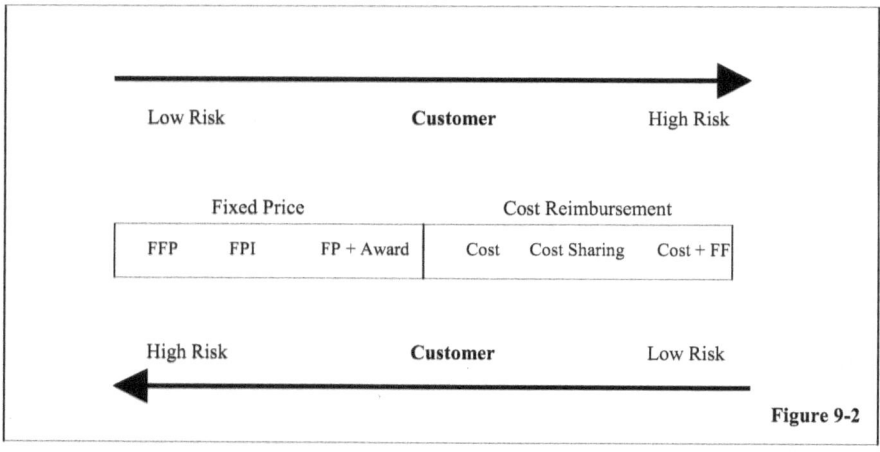

Figure 9-2

Fixed Price Contract: A fixed price contract requires that the project be completed for a fixed amount of money. The seller agrees to sell something to the buyer at a price that has been agreed to beforehand. The seller agrees to provide the buyer with something that meets the specifications as agreed, and the buyer agrees to give the seller a fixed amount of money in return. Strictly speaking, in this kind of contract, the seller must do the work specified for the agreed upon amount. In the real world, if problems occur that make it impossible for the seller to perform for the agreed upon price or the seller has severe financial problems, agreements can be modified.

In fixed price contracting, the seller is taking all of the risk of having things go wrong, but the seller is also setting the price in such a way as to be compensated for taking the risk. In fact, in this type of contract it may be that the buyer is paying more than would have been necessary if the buyer had been willing to take some of the risk.

In fixed price contracts there is no need for the buyer to know what the seller is actually spending on the project. Whether the seller spends more or less should be of no interest to the buyer. The buyer should be interested only in the specifications of the project being met.

Firm Fixed Price Contracts: In a firm fixed price contract the seller takes all of the risk. In our discussion on project risk, one of the strategies for handling risk was to deflect or transfer the risk to another organization. The most risk free way to transfer the risk is to use a firm fixed price contract. The contract terms require that the seller supply the buyer with the agreed upon goods or services at a firm fixed price. In other words, the supplier must supply the good or service without being able to recover any of the cost of doing the work if cost-increasing risks occur during the fulfillment of the contract. Frequently, in this type of contract if the supplier cannot perform for the agreed upon amount, there is some room for negotiating even after the contract has been agreed to and signed.

The firm fixed price contract has the most predictable cost of all of the types of contracts.

Fixed Price Plus Economic Adjustment Contract: In this type of contract some of the risk is kept by the buyer. All of the risks associated with the contract are borne by the seller except for the condition of changes in the economy. This type of contract can be used when there are periods of very high inflation. The contract piece is adjusted according to some formula that depends on an agreed upon economic indicator.

Fixed Price Plus Incentive Contract: In this type of contract there is an agreed upon fixed price for the project and an incentive fee for exceeding the performance of the contract. In this type of contract the buyer wishes to create some incentive for the seller. The buyer offers to increase the amount that he or she will pay for the completion of the project if the seller delivers the project early or if the project performance exceeds the agreed upon specifications.

Cost Plus Contracts: A major distinction is made between contracts that are fixed price and those that are cost reimbursable. In a cost reimbursable contract the seller agrees to perform the terms of the contract, but the buyer takes on the risk. The buyer agrees to reimburse the seller for any work that is done and for any money that is spent. When the contract is completed, the buyer pays a fixed fee to the seller for the work that was done. This is essentially the profit for doing the project.

Cost reimbursable contracts are usually done when there is a great deal of risk and uncertainty in the project or when a significant amount of investment must be made before the final results of the project can be reached.

For example, the U.S. government wants to develop a new tank for the army. The requirements are not clear, and the design of the tank must be modified to accept the latest state of the art designs for its components as it is being developed. The approval and development process may take as long as ten years. There are probably no companies that would agree to a fixed price contract for this project, so the government awards a cost plus contract instead.

In a cost plus type of contract the buyer is taking the responsibility for the risk. If problems develop in the project, the buyer will have to pay for the corrective action that is necessary. Sometimes this can actually be economical. In projects with a lot of risk, the seller usually will estimate the cost of the risks and charge the buyer enough in the price to adequately compensate for taking the risk. In a cost reimbursable contract the actual cost of the risks that occur are the only ones that are paid for.

One of the problems in a cost reimbursable contract is the determination of the actual cost. There is always the danger that the seller's report of the actual cost to the buyer may contain costs of some other projects. This means that the buyer needs to check to be sure that misallocation of cost is not occurring. In large federal government projects staffs of auditors check on correct cost reporting to ensure that this is not a problem. Many times the cost of the auditing and tracking system to ensure correct reposting makes these kinds of contracts difficult to apply unless the projects are large.

> *Cost Plus Fixed Fee Contract*: In a cost plus fixed fee contract the seller is reimbursed for all of the money that is spent meeting the contract requirements and is also paid a fixed fee. The fixed fee is essentially the profit for managing the project. Without some sort of fee in addition to the actual cost of the contract there would be no profit, and the company would simply be making the money that they spent. No company would knowingly take on this kind of contract.

> *Cost Plus Award Fee Contract*: In a cost plus award fee contract an award system is set up to compensate the seller for completing parts of the contract. The award fee can be determined by many different criteria including the quality of the workmanship, the correct filling out of reports, and practically any other criteria that are agreed to. As each of these requirements is met the award fee is determined and given to the seller.

Cost Plus Incentive Fee Contract: In a cost plus incentive fee contract an incentive system is set up for the seller to perform in excess of the agreed upon terms and specifications of the contract. Similar to a fixed price plus incentive contract, the cost plus incentive contract allows the seller to exceed the specifications and requirements of the contract. When the project is delivered early or when the design criteria and specifications have been exceeded, the incentive fee is paid.

The cost plus incentive fee contract is the least predictable of all types of contract. Not only is the variable cost of the work determined in the contract but the variable incentive that must be paid to the seller must also be considered.

10

HUMAN RESOURCES MANAGEMENT

HRM Roles and Responsibilities
Strong Matrix, Weak Matrix, and Balanced Matrix
Organizational Planning
Staff Acquisition
Team Development

Human Resources Management

Human resources is required to make the most efficient use of the project human resources. This includes all of the people involved in the project—the stakeholders of the projects, sponsors, customers, other departments, the project team, subcontractors, and all others.

Organizational planning involves organizing the human resources, establishing the roles, responsibilities, and relationships of the people that are on the project team. As in all things in project management, human resources management is done throughout the project. If at any time the project organization needs to be revised, the human resources plan will assist in carrying this out.

HRM Roles and Responsibilities

It is a long-standing joke in the project management community that if anyone ever asks who is responsible for anything in the project, the answer will always be the project manager. Truly it is easier to specify what the project manager does not do than what he or she actually does and is responsible for.

The nature and scope of the project should dictate the individual roles and responsibilities of the project team. When all of the team assignments and responsibilities have been decided, all of the functions and responsibilities of the project will have been assigned. The responsibility-accountability matrix is useful for determining and tracking the relationship between a given responsibility and who is responsible for it.

As can be seen in Figure 10-1, the responsibility-accountability matrix is a short notational form that allows us to easily see the relationship between the individuals on a project team and the responsibilities that they have. Various levels of the responsibility-accountability matrix may be developed for various parts and levels of the project.

	Dale	Jessica	John	Cathy
Requirements Definition	S	R	A	P
Functional Design	S		A	P
Detail Design	S		R	A
Development		R	S	A
Testing			S	P

Key:
P – Participates
A – Accountable
R – Reviews
I – Input required
S – Sign off

Figure 10-1

The project manager, in order to determine when activities are supposed to take place in the project, uses the project schedule (Figure 10-2). It constitutes the schedule for the work that has to be done. Of course, people are involved with the work that has to be done. The project manager in a matrix organization draws the people from the functional organization.

Task 1 [ ] Richard Thomas

Task 2 [ ] Jeanette Williams

Task 3 [ ] Nancy Brown

Figure 10-2

The functional manager must have a staffing plan that allows him or her to know where the people in their functional organization are committed. If these commitments are not organized, the utilization of the human resources will be poor. A staffing plan for the functional manager is similar to the project schedule, except that instead of showing the schedule for each task in the project, it shows the schedule for each resource in the functional manager's responsibility (Figure 10-3).

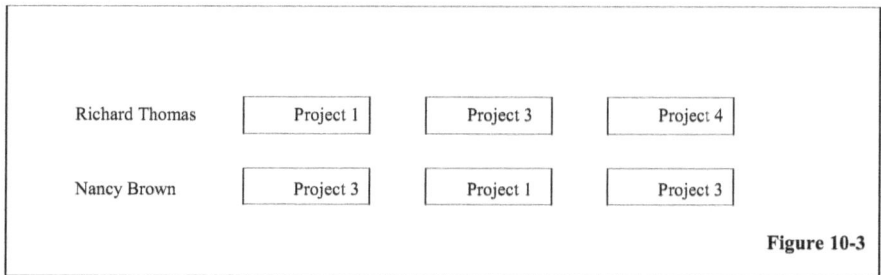

Figure 10-3

Strong Matrix, Weak Matrix, and Balanced Matrix

Strong Matrix

In a strong matrix organization the project manager has greater authority or power than the functional manager. In this condition, project managers generally get the people they want. In fact, the project managers in this type of organization get more than they should. A manager is that assertive will usually get the personnel he or she wishes. The functional manager is not able to overcome the project manager's authority and is not free to assign people where they belong and where their talent is best utilized.

If this type of organization becomes stronger, most if not all of the personnel will be working on projects, and project managers will be able to draw more highly qualified people than are really needed for their projects. The surplus personnel are bartered between the project managers themselves, bypassing the functional managers altogether. In this type of organization the project manager has strong authority (Figure 10-4).

Characteristic of Organization	Functional	Weak Matrix	Balanced Matrix	Strong Matrix	Pure Projects
Project manager power	None	Little and limited	Even with functional manager	High	Complete
Percent working full time on project	0%	0 to 25%	15 to 60%	50 to 100%	100%
Common Titles	Project coordinator Project lead	Project coordinator Project lead Project expeditor	Project manager	Project manager Program manager	Program manager Project manager

Figure 10-4

Weak Matrix

In the weak matrix organization, the project manager does not have as much power as the functional manager. This problem usually occurs in organizations that are moving into matrix management for the first time. The situation occurs something like this: The chief executive office (CEO) of the company decides that matrix management is the thing for the company to do. Almost overnight an attempt is made to change the organization from a functional organization to a matrix management.

When this attempt is made, there is a reaction from the functional managers. Actually, there should be a reaction. After all, these are the major human assets in the company. They would not be in a position of authority if they were not good managers.

The functional managers see the problem in the new organization. In the past they had responsibility for the administrative as well as the directing of work in their part of the organization. Under matrix management they no longer direct some of the work that their people are doing. The project manager directs the work. This is a threat to the functional managers. The salary that the company is going to pay the project managers is going to come from someplace. Most likely it is going to come from cuts in functional manager's pay. The functional managers react by convincing the upper management of the company to only allow the project managers to recommend work to be done, and the functional managers will continue to actually direct the work.

This form of matrix management can be used if there is a transition going on. In the beginning of the transition to matrix management, the project managers are new and inexperienced. As the project managers gain experience, they should be given more authority over the people who report to them. As the same time, the functional managers can be transitioned out of the organization and promoted into higher and more responsible jobs. As the functional managers move on, they can be replaced by the more appropriate administrative manager, and more of the direction of work can be done by the project manager.

Balanced Matrix

In this type of organization, the power levels of the functional manager and the project manager are more in balance. This means that the functional manager cannot force the project manager, and the project manager cannot force the functional manager. The functional manager makes the decisions about where the people in his or her department are assigned, and the project manager works with the functional manager to recruit the proper person for the project assignment.

A balancing rule can be applied. By setting a specific interval of time as a requirement for moving a person to the project team, balance can be achieved. Or example, a person who is required to work full time on a project for two months is transferred to the project, while a person who is required to work less time than two months remains in his or her functional department. The person working more than two months is physically moved to the project space, and he or she returns to the functional area when the work is completed. The person working less than two months on the project remains under the supervision of the functional manager. The project manager authorizes the work to be done in the functional area by generating a work order or some other device.

By adjusting the balance point, more or less work can be made to happen in the functional areas. If more work is being handled in the project, the project manager has more people reporting to him or her, and the project manager's power level is increased. At one extreme, we have a strong matrix where the length of time required moving a person to the project team is very short. At the other extreme, we have a weak matrix where the length of time required moving a person to the project team is very long.

How to Make Matrix Management to Work

Matrix management is not without its problems. This kind of organization is quite complex in comparison to the functional or pure project types of organization. Since the resources are shared, people working in this type of organization also share their bosses. This increases problems in communications, and many ore management skills are required to make it all work.

These problems are all offset by the flexibility that is achieved. The matrix organization is able to respond quickly and correctly to the needs of the customer in a proper fashion. The project team has focus on the customer's needs. Good project direction and participative management lead to high motivation and a sense of achievement and recognition on the project team.

Moving from a functional organization to a matrix organization may take two or three years in some organizations. This is necessary because it takes time to move the functional managers out of their positions and into other productive areas. If movement from functional organizations to matrix organizations is too fast, the result can be chaos and the loss of important personnel. The objective must be to create the impression that people are going to be promoted to other positions and not that their position is going to be degraded. The functional managers in the existing organization are the major assets of the company and must not be lost.

Personnel and Personal Evaluations

It is critically important that functional managers and project managers work together to evaluate employees. This is a problem because the project team members may be assigned to the project for only a short time, and they may be assigned to several different projects with several different project managers during the course of the evaluation period. Project managers are oriented toward the goals of the project and frequently think of employee evaluations as administrative work that is the responsibility of the functional manager.

One simple method for accomplishing this and solve the problem is to have the project manager or subproject manager meet individually with people on their project team and review progress being made toward their project assignments. Something as simple as a lined tablet can be used for this. The project manager meets with an individual and makes notes on the tablet. When the meeting is over, a copy of the notes is given to the individual and a copy is filed away by the project manager.

When the person leaves the project, the notes are reviewed by the individual and the project manager, a summary is written by the project manager with comments by the individual, and the whole package is copied and sent to the functional manager. In this way, when the time of appraisal is due the functional manager has the notes from the project managers and can make a proper evaluation of the employees.

Organizational Planning

Organizational planning involves identifying, documenting, and assigning project roles, responsibilities, and reporting relationships. Roles, responsibilities, and reporting relationships may be assigned to individuals or to groups. The individuals and groups may be part of the organization performing the project, or they may be external to it. Internal groups are often associated with a specific functional department such as engineering, marketing, or accounting.

On most projects, the majority of organizational planning is done as part of the earliest project phases. However, the results of this process should be reviewed regularly throughout the project to ensure continued applicability. If the initial organization is no longer effective, then it should be revised promptly.

Organizational planning is often tightly linked with communications planning, since the project's organizational structure will have a major effect on the project's communications requirements.

Staff Acquisition

Staff acquisition involves getting the needed human resources (individuals or groups) assigned to and working on the project. In most environments, the "best" resources may not be available, and the project management team must take care to ensure that the resources that are available will meet project requirements.

Team Development

Team development includes both enhancing the ability of stakeholders to contribute as individuals as well as enhancing the ability of the team to function as a team. Individual development (managerial and technical) is the foundation necessary to develop the team. Development as a team is critical to the project's ability to meet its objectives.

Team development on a project is often complicated when individual team members are accountable to both a functional manager and the project manager. Effective management of this dual reporting relationship is often a critical success factor for the project, and is generally the responsibility of the project manager.

11

PROFESSIONAL RESPONSIBILITIES

PMP Code of Professional Conduct

PMP Code of Professional Conduct

As a PMI® Project Management Professional (PMP®), I agree to support and adhere to the responsibilities described in the PMP Code of Conduct.

I. Responsibilities to the Profession

A. *Compliance with all Organizational Rules and Policies*

1. Responsibility to provide accurate and truthful representations concerning all information directly or indirectly related to all aspects of the PMI Certification Program, including and not limited to the following: examination applications, test item banks, examinations, answer sheets, candidate information, and professional development program reporting forms.
2. Upon a reasonable and clear factual basis, responsibility to report possible violations of the PMP Code of Professional Conduct by individuals in the field of project management.
3. Responsibility to cooperate with PMI concerning ethics violations and the collection of related information.
4. Responsibility to disclose to clients, customers, owners, or contractors, significant circumstances that could be construed as a conflict of interest, or an appearance of impropriety.

B. *Candidate/Certificant Professional Practice*

1. Responsibility to provide accurate, truthful advertising and representations concerning qualifications, experience, and performance of services.
2. Responsibility to comply with laws, regulations, and ethical standards governing professional practice in the state/province and/or country when providing project management services.

C. *Advancement of the Profession*

1. Responsibility to recognize and respect intellectual property developed or owned by others, and to otherwise act in an accurate, truthful, and complete manner, including all activities related to professional work and research.
2. Responsibility to support and disseminate the PMP Code of Professional Conduct to other PMI certificants.

II. Responsibilities to Customers and the Public

A. *Qualifications, Experience, and Performance of Professional Services*
1. Responsibility to provide accurate and truthful representations to the public in advertising, public statements, and in the preparation of estimates concerning costs, services, and expected results.
2. Responsibility to maintain and satisfy the scope and objectives of professional services, unless otherwise directed by the customer.
3. Responsibility to maintain and respect the confidentiality of sensitive information obtained in the course of professional activities or otherwise where a clear obligation exists.

B. *Conflict of Interest Situations and Other Prohibited Professional Conduct*
1. Responsibility to ensure that a conflict of interest does not compromise legitimate interests of a client or customer, or influence/interfere with professional judgments.
2. Responsibility to refrain from offering or accepting inappropriate payments, gifts, or other forms of compensation for personal gain, unless in conformity with applicable laws or customs of the country where project management services are being provided.

APPENDIX

Exercise Questions and Answers
Summary of Project Management Knowledge Areas

Exercise Questions and Answers

The following questions are examples of the type of questions that appear on the PMP® Certification Examination.

1. The **MAJOR** processes for project integration management are:

    A. Project plan development, project plan execution, and overall change control.
    B. Project plan development, project plan execution, and scope change control.
    C. Project plan development, overall change control, and scope change control.
    D. Project plan development, initiation, and overall change control.

2. Project sponsors have the **GREATEST** influence on the scope, quality, time, and cost of the project during the:

    A. Concept phase.
    B. Development phase.
    C. Execution phase.
    D. Close-down phase.

3. Ideally, communication between the project manager and the project team members should take place:

    A. Via daily status reports.

B. Through approved documented forms.

C. By written and oral communication.

D. Through the formal chain of command.

4. A project's payback period ends when:

    A. Profit maximum is realized.

    B. Unit profit is realized.

    C. Monthly revenue exceeds monthly costs.

    D. Cumulative revenue equals cumulative costs.

5. A scope statement is important because it:

    A. Provides the basis for making future project decisions.

    B. Provides a brief summary of the project.

    C. Approves the project for the stakeholders.

    D. Provides criteria for measuring project cost.

6. A project management professional can compare earned value performance data to all of the following project management tools **EXCEPT**:

    A. Critical path analysis.

    B. Technical performance metrics.

    C. Risk mitigation plans.

    D. Forecasted final costs and schedule estimates.

7. During the project scope planning process, the work breakdown structure should be developed to:

   A. The sub-project level.
   B. The level determined by the project office.
   C. A level allowing for adequate estimates.
   D. The cost center level.

8. The decomposition process is a technique used to construct a:

   A. Precedence network.
   B. Critical Path Method Diagram.
   C. Variance analysis.
   D. Work breakdown structure.

9. A project loses a contractor in the middle of a project. A new project team is formed to replace the role of the lost contractor and his/her team. As a project manager, what is the **FIRST** topic to address to the team in the kick-off meeting?

   A. Identify team roles and responsibilities.
   B. Review detailed schedule.
   C. Discuss cost estimates.
   D. Emphasize your authority.

10.   Constructive team roles include:

A. Encourager, initiator, and gatekeeper.

B. Information giver, devil's advocate, and clarifier.

C. Withdrawer, harmonizer, and blocker.

D. Summarizer, recognition seeker, and information seeker.

11.   A project schedule completion date will change if:

A. The critical path is reduced.

B. The contingency is no longer available.

C. No float time is available.

D. Project resources are reduced.

12.   Your project is behind schedule due to conflict between team members. Having resolved the conflict, to get the project back on schedule, you should consider:

A. Crashing the schedule.

B. Performing resource leveling.

C. Conducting reverse resource allocation scheduling.

D. Utilizing the critical chair resources.

13.   Risk quantification includes:

A. Enumerating sources of internal and external events.

B. Identifying potential events and impact.

C. Evaluating probability and impact.

D. Developing contingency plans and resources.

14.   In which project phase do you have the **GREATEST** influence on project risk?

A. Conceptual.

B. Design.

C. Execution.

D. Implementation.

15.   A precise description of a deliverable is called a:

A. Specification.

B. Baseline.

C. Work package.

D. Work breakdown structure element.

16.   The objective of fast tracking a project is to:

A. Increase productivity.

B. Reduce project duration.

C. Increase schedule tracking controls.

D. Reduce project risks.

17.   When a project manager places a purchase order for a piece of equipment, it represents which of the following?

    A. Commitment.

    B. Expense.

    C. Cash out-flow.

    D. Capital investment.

18.   Which of the following are frequently used tools in procurement planning?

    A. Make or buy analysis, expert judgment, and contract type selection.

    B. Contract type selection, bidders conferences, and expert judgment.

    C. Expert judgment, audits, and bidders conferences.

    D. Make or buy analysis, contract type selection, and weighting system.

19.   You have just taken control of a project in the middle of execution and need to learn who has approval authority for revisions in scope. Which document provides this information?

    A. Resource assignment matrix.

    B. Change control plan.

    C. Project charter.

    D. Client organization chart.

20. Of the following conflict management approaches, which is believed to lead to the **LEAST** enduring positive results?

A. Problem solving.
B. Avoidance.
C. Compromise.
D. Forcing.

21. Complex projects, involving cross-disciplinary efforts, are **MOST** effectively managed by:

A. Multiple lead project managers.
B. A functional organization.
C. A strong matrix organization.
D. A strong traditional manager.

22. The measure used to forecast project cost at completion is:

A. CPI.
B. SPI.
C. BCWP.
D. ACWP.

23.   A contractor's deliverable has been delayed 30 days. The process of determining how this event will affect the project schedule is called risk:

A. Identification.
B. Mitigation.
C. Simulation.
D. Assessment.

24.   Conflict resolution techniques that may be used on a project include:

A. Withdrawing, compromising, controlling, and forcing.
B. Controlling, forcing, smoothing, and withdrawing.
C. Confronting, compromising, smoothing, and directing.
D. Smoothing, confronting, forcing, and withdrawing.

25.   It is critical for your company to offer its products on the Internet to increase its market share. The company has no previous experience in this area, but it believes that knowledge is needed rapidly. As you have shown an interest in the Internet, you are asked to start planning for this project. What is the **FIRST** step to take as you begin planning?

A. Identify the risks.
B. Plan the scope.
C. Establish a resource plan.
D. Complete a cost and schedule estimate.

26. Effective stakeholder management includes all of the following project elements **EXCEPT:**

   A. Clear requirements definition.
   B. Scope change control.
   C. Timely status information.
   D. Frequent cost reports.

27. A likely result of using "compromise" to resolve a two-party conflict is:

   A. Lose-lose.
   B. Win-lose.
   C. Win-win.
   D. Lose-win.

28. As part of the quality audit, the scope statement is checked against the work results to ensure the conformance to the customer requirements. The results should be documented and used for:

   A. Estimating future projects.
   B. Changing the project scope.
   C. Defining future project tasks.
   D. Validating the quality process.

29.   A generally accepted method to confirm accuracy of task progress is through:

A. Earned value.

B. Probability vs. outcome.

C. Maximum ceiling.

D. Work breakdown structure.

30.   Which of the following techniques is used to control the project schedule?

A. Pareto diagram

B. Performance measurement

C. Parametric modeling

D. Statistical sampling

31.   Pareto analysis, cause and effect, and flow charts are all tools used in quality:

A. Control.

B. Benchmarking.

C. Planning.

D. Verification.

32.   Elements of changing a project schedule include all of the follow-
       ing **EXCEPT**:

A. Obtain the appropriate levels of approval.
B. Submit the appropriate change requests.
C. Evaluate the impact of a change to the schedule.
D. Adjust the project end date to the schedule variance.

33.   An individual's willingness to take a risk can be determined by:

A. Decision tree modeling.
B. Monte Carlo method.
C. Sensitivity analysis.
D. Utility function.

34.   All of the following assist in determining the impact of a scope
       change **EXCEPT**:

A. Project charter.
B. Baseline.
C. Performance measurement.
D. Milestones.

35.   A project was estimated to cost $1.5 million and scheduled to last
       six months. After three months, the earned value analysis shows
       the following:

BCWP = $650,000
BCWS = $750,000
ACWP = $800,000
What are the schedule and cost variances?

A. SV= +$100,000 / CV= +$150,000

B. SV= +$150,000 / CV= -$100,000

C. SV= -$50,000 / CV= +$150,000

D. SV= -$100,000 / CV= -$150,000

36.   Configuration management is a technique for:

A. Overall change control.

B. Project plan execution.

C. Scope planning.

D. Risk quantification.

37.   Scope change control **MUST** be integrated with all of the following control processes **EXCEPT:**

A. Schedule.

B. Cost.

C. Procurement.

D. Quality.

198 • Project Management Handbook

38.   Reviewing work products and results to ensure that all were completed satisfactorily and formally accepted is part of:

A. Risk management.
B. Quality control.
C. Change control management.
D. Scope verification.

39.   Risk response development is intended to:

A. Create steps to identify project risks.
B. Formulate strategies for dealing with adverse events.
C. Construct a list of previous project risks.
D. Develop measurements to quantify project risks.

40.   Due to cuts in funding, your project has been terminated. The scope verification process:

A. Should be delayed until the project is completed.
B. Should determine the correctness of the work results.
C. Should establish and document the level and extent of completion.
D. Will form the basis of the project audit.

41.   During the contract close-out, the project manager needs to document the:

A. Formal acceptance.

B. Statement of work.

C. Payment schedule.

D. Change control procedure.

42. You've been engaged to manage a project. The estimated cost of the project is $1,000,000. The project sponsor has approved this amount. Your earned value calculations indicate that the project will be completed on time and under budget by $200,000. Based on this calculation, your personal profit will decrease by $2,000. At the completion of this project, the project manager will document and archive all project information. This information may be used for future projects in all areas **EXCEPT:**

A. Estimating durations.

B. Administering contracts.

C. Resolving conflicts.

D. Allocating resources.

43. A **KEY** activity in closing out a project is to:

A. Disseminate status reports and risk assessments.

B. Disseminate information to formalize project completion.

C. Monitor the specific project results to determine if they comply with relevant quality standards.

D. Transfer all the project records to the project owners.

44. You've been engaged to manage a project. The estimated cost of the project is $1,000,000. The project sponsor has approved this amount. Your earned value calculations indicate that the project will be completed on time and under budget by $200,000. Based on this calculation, your personal profit will decrease by $2,000. Given the estimated decrease in personal profit, what action should you take?

A. Invoice for the full $1,000,000 based on the contract.

B. Add tasks to improve the outcome and increase the actual project cost.

C. Inform the end-user that you can add features to the project in order to use the entire budget.

D. Communicate the projected financial outcome to the project sponsor.

45. You are building a water treatment facility. Routine tests reveal that there are contaminants in the water but that they have an extremely low risk for causing any sickness. As the project manager, you should:

A. Inform the public that a detailed examination has been ordered to determine the extent to which the problem exists.

B. Do nothing because there is extremely low risk for sickness except for some effects on small children and the elderly.

C. Tell the public there is no problem, except for small children and the elderly who need to boil the water before drinking.

D. Educate the public about the advances on water treatment technology and the industry efficiency and safety record.

46.   A **KEY** activity for achieving customer satisfaction is to define:

A. The business use.

B. Requirements.

C. Product specificity.

D. Change control.

47.   When it appears that a design error will interfere with meeting technical performance objectives, the **PREFERRED** response is to:

A. Decrease the performance value to equal the assessed value.

B. Develop alternative solutions to the problem.

C. Increase the specified value to set a new performance goal.

D. Reduce the overall technical complexity of the project.

48.   The disorientation experienced by people who suddenly find themselves living and working in a different environment is known as:

A. Culture shock.

B. Sociocentrism.

C. Temporal shock.

D. Ethnocentrism.

202 • Project Management Handbook

49. What is the **MOST** effective process to ensure that cultural and ethical differences do not impede success of your multi-national project?

A. Co-locating.
B. Training.
C. Forming.
D. Teaming.

50. Negotiating across international cultures involves mutual interdependence between parties. The negotiating **MUST** be conducted in an atmosphere of:

A. Mutual trust and cooperation
B. Generalities and vagueness
C. Sincerity and compassion
D. Uncertainty and caution

Answers to Sample Examination Questions

Question Number	Performance Domain	Answer
1	Initiating	A
2	Initiating	A
3	Initiating	C
4	Initiating	D
5	Planning	A
6	Planning	D
7	Planning	C

8	Planning	D
9	Planning	A
10	Planning	A
11	Planning	A
12	Planning	A
13	Planning	C
14	Planning	A
15	Planning	A
16	Planning	B
17	Executing	A
18	Executing	A
19	Executing	B
20	Executing	B
21	Executing	C
22	Executing	A
23	Executing	D
24	Executing	D
25	Executing	B
26	Executing	D
27	Executing	A
28	Executing	C
29	Controlling	A
30	Controlling	B
31	Controlling	A
32	Controlling	D
33	Controlling	D
34	Controlling	A
35	Controlling	D
36	Controlling	A
37	Controlling	C
38	Controlling	D
39	Controlling	B

40	Closing	C
41	Closing	A
42	Closing	C
43	Closing	B
44	Professional Responsibility	D
45	Professional Responsibility	A
46	Professional Responsibility	B
47	Professional Responsibility	B
48	Professional Responsibility	A
49	Professional Responsibility	B
50	Professional Responsibility	A

Summary of Project Management Knowledge Areas

The Process of Project Management

Projects are composed of processes. A process is "a series of actions bringing about a result". Project processes are performed by people and generally fall into one of the two major categories: (1) *Project management processes*; and (2) *Product-oriented processes*.

Project management processes describe, organize and complete the work of the project. Product-oriented processes specify and create the project's product. Product-oriented processes are typically defined by the project life cycle and vary by application area.

Project management processes and product-oriented processes overlap and interact throughout the project. For example, the scope of the project cannot be defined in the absence of some basic understanding of how to create the product.

Integration Management

Project Integration Management includes the processes required to ensure that the various elements of the project are properly coordinated. It involves making tradeoffs among competing objectives and alternatives to meet or exceed stakeholder(s) needs and expectations.

Quality Management:

One of the most important aspects of project management is quality management. It is what holds a project together. One must have excellent quality in the projects that are being produced or provided. Quality management is the process that ensures that we produce each of the deliverables of the project. The three areas of quality management that we are concerned with are *Quality Planning, Quality Assurance,* and *Quality Control.*

The cost of quality is actually the profit of quality. The cost of preventing quality problems is less than the cure of having to correct the problem once it has happened. The savings that are realized in a good quality management plan are more than offsetting the cost of its implementation.

Quality control is the implementation of various control techniques. Various inspection techniques are implemented to prevent defects in processes as well as to prevent the customer from receiving parts that are defective. The Acceptable Quality Level (AQL) is the allowed number of defective parts that can be delivered without the entire batch or lot being considered to be bad. This is because trying to produce 100 percent perfect parts becomes very expensive as the 100 percent mark is neared. Buyer's risk is the risk that a lot of parts that are unacceptable will be accepted by sampling inspection. Seller's risk is the possibility that a lot or batch of parts that is truly acceptable will be rejected.

Sampling inspection is a statistical method of inspecting large numbers of parts. It is based on the probability that if there is a certain percentage of defects in a large lot the probability of finding them can be determined statistically.

The area of quality is one of the areas in which a remarkable amount of money can be saved. This is because we not only save the direct and observable cost of defective goods and services to our customers, but also we save in lost goodwill and future problems that defects bring about.

In the area of project management, we must be vigilant that we hold to good quality standards at all times, because failure to adhere to good quality practices could end with the ruination of the organization.

Project Management Institute (PMI) takes the position in the *Guide to the PMBOK* that the knowledge areas for study of quality are focused in the area of what I call "factory" quality control techniques rather than the concepts of Total Quality Management (TQM) that are more popular today.

In preparing for the PMP examination, it is advisable to study additionally in the area of TQM since the certification exam committee may feel that this is an appropriate area for project management regardless of the treatment in the *PMBOK.*

Scope Management:

The most common reason for project failure is not clearly identifying exactly what is to be delivered by the project. The project charter is a device that helps getting project off the ground and headed in the right direction. It allows the project manager to express his/her understanding of the project and what its accomplishments are intended to be.

Further, all of the stakeholders in the project must be identified. A stakeholder is any person or group that has direct or indirect interest in carrying out the project. The project team, the customer(s), the management of your firm, and many others are or can be stakeholders.

The project manager must have input into the pricing of the project. The price should not be determined by the cost of the project; however the cost of the project is a very real and important consideration in making sure that the project benefits are high enough to justify the cost.

The scope baseline is the first of the three baselines that measure project success. Without the scope baseline it is not possible for the cost and schedule baseline to be meaningful.

The work breakdown structure is the heart of the project. From the work breakdown structure, it is possible to determine the detailed definitions of the work that has to be done in the project. It is the basis for making a bottom-up estimate and for producing the project schedule.

Change management is initiated as soon as it is practical in the definition of the scope of work for the project. It must be implemented by the time the scope baseline is defined. From that point on, all changes to the project scope should be traceable to an authorized change.

All projects must be justified. There are many justification methods for projects. With the exception of mandated projects, projects are justified on the basis of cost versus benefits. Today, because of the availability of sophisticated, fast computers the internal rate of return on investment, or IRR, has become the most popular method of financial justification of projects.

Cost and Time Management:

Cost management is a necessary part of project management, for it makes it possible to manage the cost baseline of the project. Without cost management, projects would use more or less money than allocated, and it would be impossible to fund future projects. The project manager, as in all things, is the person responsible for project cost management.

The work breakdown structure is the basis for the cost estimate. Since the work breakdown structure identifies all of the project work in a detailed workable way, it becomes the best place to determine the cost of the project. A cost estimate that has been prepared this way produces a detailed estimate, which can be rolled bottom-up to any level of detail desired.

Cost estimating is done over the life of the project. In the beginning of the project only a small amount of information is known about the project, thus, there may be some inaccurate estimates produced.

Cost control in project management is best achieved through the use of the earned value reporting system. This reporting system makes it possible to measure performance to schedule and performance to budget in the same system. Project performance over or under budget is measured in dollars. Project performance ahead or behind schedule is in dollars as well.

In addition to the earned value reporting system, the project manager must face many of the financial decisions that a small business manager must face and be aware of the financial world of reporting.

Time management in a project produces the schedule baseline. The activities of the project must be defined before they can be scheduled. There is a one-to-one relationship between the activities described at the bottom of the work breakdown structure and the activities that are scheduled in the project schedule. Activity durations for the schedule are determined in the estimating process or phase.

The activities are sequenced in the logical order in which they are performed. This logical ordering is represented in a network diagram. The network diagramming method that is used today is the precedence diagram. With the use of the correct logical relationship and the leads and lags, every logical relationship in the schedule can be diagrammed.

Fast tracking and crashing are two techniques for reducing schedules that must have a promise date sooner than predicted by the schedule. Buffering is a technique for increasing schedules that can have a promise date later than the date predicted by the schedule.

The critical path method is a method of managing a project by applying the management effort of the project manager and the efforts of the project team in the most effective way. Activities with little or no float or tolerance are given more attention than activities with float or great amount of tolerance.

Program Evaluation and Review Technique, or PERT, is a technique that is used to predict project completions when there is a great deal of uncertainty in the estimated durations. PERT makes a statistical approximation of the project completion by using the estimate for the optimistic, pessimistic, and most likely duration for each task.

The Monte Carlo simulation is used to eliminate a problem associated with PERT. The problem is that the critical path may move from activity to activity under different conditions. Monte Carlo is a simulation technique that runs many schedules with selected durations, and statistically calculates the effect of variable durations and reports (statistically) the results.

Communications Management:

Whenever project management is discussed by project managers it is not very long before the topic of communications comes up. Communications management is the process that allows for the timely and appropriate generation of information.

The communications model consists of a sender and a receiver. The sender thinks of what must be communicated, encodes the communication, and transmits it to the receiver. The receiver perceives the message, decodes it, and understands the meaning of the message, if there is insufficient meaning in the message, the receiver can (and should) communicate feedback to the sender.

There are many barriers to communications. These inhibit the communication from occurring in an optimal and effective way. The barriers can be overcome by using good communication techniques.

There are many types of communications and there are many channels through which communications flow. Verbal and nonverbal communications are appropriate at some times and not others. It is important that the proper type of communication be used. The same method for communicating that may work well in one situation may not work in another.

Formal and informal communications are important in project management. Many times the project manager is required to make formal presentations to customers and stakeholders in the project. Good presentation skills are essential to good managers.

The other *half* of communication is *listening*. A good project manager must also be a good listener. These can be improved by following good listening habits.

Network techniques and management by walking around allow for the collection of good and valuable information.

One of the problems that occurred in project management when matrix management was first tried was performance-reviews being mishandled by project managers. Performance reviews of everyone on the project team are extremely important and necessary. These reviews can be a simple as both the manager and the subordinate periodically adding their comments to a sheet of paper and making copies for one another.

Risk Management:

Risk management has become one of the most important aspects of project management. As companies become better at managing projects, the significance of risk management is becoming more important. Many companies are not yet adept at determining project cost and schedule and scope baselines and have not yet learned to manage the work that is actually going to be in the project. Until this is satisfactorily performed, it is not worthwhile to consider the next step. This step or process is risk management.

The components of risk identification, probability, and impact must all be considered in order to determine how a risk should be dealt with. The combination of impact and probability determine the severity of the risk. The severity of a risk determines its importance in ranking it among other risks. The steps in risk management—risk identification, risk evaluation, risk mitigation, and risk control—are necessary to manage risk. The steps must be carried out on a continuous basis throughout the project.

Companies and individuals have risk tolerances. They either tend to be gamblers and are willing to take chances to achieve rewards, or they tend to be conservative and less willing to take chances.

Various methods can be used for risk identification. All of the techniques that are useful for group dynamics are also useful for identifying risks. Risk evaluation must determine the probability of the risk occurring and the impact that it will have if it occurs. Risks that are either very low in probability or very low in impact need not be considered a serious threat to the project even though they may be coupled with high impacts or high probability, respectively.

Expected values for risks are useful in determining the quantitative value of a risk in terms of dollars. The expected value of a risk is the approximate amount of money that could be spent to eliminate the risk.

Once it has been determined that a risk should be dealt with, the proper strategy must be employed. Risk can be avoided by completely eliminating the possibility of the risk through redesign or restructure of the project. Risks can be transferred by making someone else outside the project responsible for the risk. Risks can be mitigated by reducing either their probability or impact to an acceptable level.

Contingency reserves are monies set aside for dealing with an identified risk when it occurs. The contingency reserve is part of the project budget; however, it is a passive budget. Management reserves are monies that are set aside for dealing with unidentified risks when they occur. Management reserves are part of the project budget.

Procurement and Contract Management:

Many times a project is not able to produce everything that is needed to complete the process. When this occurs, the project manager becomes the client of another project manager, and the roles are somewhat reversed from their usual state.

The project manager now becomes the purchaser. It is important that the project manager understands the purchasing cycle and the basics of contracting. It is quite easy to find ourselves with a significant problem with no legal protection. Contracts provide us with a formal agreement that is binding between the two or more parties involved and are enforceable by our legal system and courts.

There are many reasons why we may not wish to produce something ourselves. This is known as a make or buy decision. Many factors affect these decisions.

The contract life cycle is similar to the project life cycle in that requirements are developed, requisitions are generated, vendors are contracted and solicited, and finally one is selected and awarded the contract. Once the award is made, the project manager must manage this contractor just as if he/she were part of the project team.

There are many types of contracts. The various types of contracts can be explained by considering them in light of risk and who accepts the risk. Fixed price types of contracts have an agreement to pay a fixed price for some specified good or service. The risk here is on the side of seller. If anything happens that increases the cost of producing the good or service, the seller most likely must bear the additional cost without being able to increase the selling price to the buyer. In cost plus types of contracts, the buyer is willing to reimburse the seller for any reasonable costs that have occurred. The risk of increased cost due to unforeseen problems is borne likely by the buyer.

When we purchase goods and services for projects, many different purchasing arrangements can be made. Forward buying and blanket ordering are methods that are used to make a mutually beneficial and acceptable arrangement for both the buyer and the seller.

Human Resources Management:

The purpose of human resources management in project management is to make the most effective use of the human resources involved in the project. As always, the project manager is responsible for the human resources management of the project.

Projects work best when the environment around them is organized in a way that is appropriate for project management. The matrix organization is best for project management, because it allows for the flexibility necessary when managing companies on a project basis.

Project teams must be motivated. Much of the research that has been recently conducted on the theories of motivation relates favorably to the management techniques that are fundamental to project management. These motivating methods favor participative management, responsibility and accountability, and recognition for work done well. The concepts of job enlargement and job enhancement fit well into the project management methodology.

In order to be an effective project manager, one must have skills in dealing with the normal conflicts occur from day to day within the project team and between the project team and those external to the project team. Understanding the use of power is necessary for the success of the project.

A project manager spends much of his/her time in meetings. Therefore, it is important that meetings be efficient, effective, and productive. Meeting agendas allow people to properly prepare themselves for meetings and help participants focus on the subjects that they are supposed to discuss.

Process Groups / Knowledge Area	Initiating	Planning	Executing	Controlling	Closing
Project Integration Management		Project Plan Development	Project Plan Execution	Integrated Change Control	
Project Scope Management	Initiation	Scope Planning Scope Definition		Scope Verification Scope Change Control	
Project Time Management		Activity Definition Activity Sequencing Activity Duration Estimating Schedule Development		Schedule Control	
Project Cost Management		Resource Planning Cost Estimating Cost Budgeting		Cost Control	
Project Quality Management		Quality Planning	Quality Assurance	Quality Control	
Project Human Resources Management		Organizational Planning Staff Acquisition	Team Development		
Project Communications Management		Communications Planning	Information Distribution	Performance Reporting	Administrative Closure
Risk Project Management		Risk Management Planning Risk Identification Qualitative Risk Analysis Quantitative Risk Analysis Risk Response Planning		Risk Monitoring	
Project Procurement Management		Procurement Planning Solicitation Planning	Solicitation Source Selection Contract Administration		Contract Closure

Mapping of Project Management Processes to the Process Groups and Knowledge Areas

GLOSSARY

I.   INCLUSIONS AND EXCLUSIONS

This glossary includes terms that are:

- Unique or nearly unique to project management (e.g., scope statement, work package, work breakdown structure, critical path method).
- Not unique to project management, but used differently or with a narrower meaning in project management than in general everyday usage (e.g., early start date, activity, task).

This glossary generally does not include the following:

- Application area-specific terms (e.g., project prospectus as a legal document—unique to real estate development).
- Terms whose use in project management does not differ in any material way from everyday use (e.g., calendar).
- Compound terms whose meaning are clear from combined meanings of the component parts.
- Variants when the meaning of the variant is clear from the base term (e.g., exception report is included, exception reporting is not).

As a result of the above inclusions and exclusions, this glossary includes the following:

- A preponderance of terms related to Project Scope Management, Project Time Management, and Project Risk Management, since many of the terms used in these knowledge areas are unique or nearly unique to project management.
- Many terms from Project Quality Management, since these terms are used narrowly than in their everyday usage.

215

- Relatively few terms related to Project Human Resources Management and Project Communications Management, since most of the terms used in these knowledge areas have narrow meanings that are unique to a particular application area.

II.   COMMON ACRONYMS

AC	Actual Cost
ACWP	Actual Cost of Work Performed
AD	Activity Description
ADM	Arrow Diagramming Method
AF	Actual Finish date
AOA	Activity-on-Arrow
AON	Activity-on-Node
AS	Actual Start date
BAC	Budget at Completion
BCWP	Budgeted Cost of Work Performed
BCWS	Budgeted Cost of Work Scheduled
CAP	Control Account Plan (aka Cost Account Plan)
CCB	Change Control Board
CPFF	Cost-Plus-Fixed-Fee
CPI	Cost Performance Index
CPIF	Cost-Plus-Incentive-Fee
CPM	Critical Path Method
CV	Cost Variance
DD	Data Date
DU	Duration
EAC	Estimate at Completion
EF	Early Finish date
ES	Early Start date
ETC	Estimate to Complete
EV	Earned Value
EVM	Earned Value Management
FF	Free Float or Finish-to-Finish
FFP	Firm Fixed-Price

FPIF	Fixed-Price-Incentive-Fee
FS	Finish-to-Start
GERT	Graphical Evaluation and Review Technique
IFB	Invitation for Bid
LF	Late Finish date
LOE	Level of Effort
LS	Late Start date
OBS	Organization(al) Breakdown Structure
PC	Percent Complete
PDM	Precedence Diagramming Method
PERT	Program Evaluation and Review Technique
PF	Planned Finish date
PM	Project Management or Project Manager
PMBOK	Project Management Body of Knowledge
PMP	Project Management Professional
PS	Planned Start date
PV	Planned Value
QA	Quality Assurance
QC	Quality Control
RAM	Responsibility Assignment Matrix
RDU	Remaining Duration
RFP	Request for Proposal
RFQ	Request for Quotation or Request for Qualification
SF	Scheduled Finish date or Start-to-Finish
SOW	Statement of Work
SPI	Schedule Performance Index
SS	Scheduled Start date or Start-to-Start
SV	Schedule Variance
TC	Target Completion date
TF	Total Float or Target Finish date
TQM	Total Quality Management
TS	Target Start date
VE	Value Engineering
WBS	Work Breakdown Structure

III. DEFINITIONS

Many of the words defined here have broader, and in some cases different, dictionary definitions.

The definitions use the following conventions:

- Terms used as part of the definitions and that are defined in the glossary are shown in *italics*.

- When synonyms are included, no definition is given and the reader is directed to the preferred term (e.g., *see preferred term*).

Accountability Matrix	See responsibility assignment matrix.
Activity	An element of work performed during the course of a project. An activity normally has an expected duration, an expected cost, and expected resource requirements. Activities can be subdivided into tasks.
Activity Definition	Identifying the specific activities that must be performed to produce the various project deliverables.
Activity Description (AD)	A short phrase or label used in a project network diagram. The activity description normally describes the scope of work of the activity.
Activity Duration Estimating	Estimating the number of work periods that will be needed to complete individual activities.
Activity-on-Arrow (AOA)	See arrow diagramming method.
Activity-on-Node (AON)	See precedence diagramming method.
Activity Sequencing	Identifying and documenting interactivity logical relationships.
Actual Cost (AC)	Total costs incurred that must relate to whatever cost was budgeted within the planned value and earned value (which can sometimes be direct labor hours alone, direct costs alone, or all costs including indirect costs) in accomplishing work during a given time period. See also earned value.
Actual Cost of Work Performed (ACWP)	This term has been replaced with the term actual cost.
Actual Finish date (AF)	The point in time that work actually ended on an activity. (Note: In some application areas, the activity is considered "finished" when work is "substantially complete.")
Actual Start date (AS)	The point in time that work actually started on an activity.
Administrative Closure	Generating, gathering, and disseminating information to formalize phase or project completion.
Application Area	A category of projects that have common elements not present in all projects. Application areas are usually defined in terms of either the product of the project (i.e., by similar technologies or industry sectors) or the type of customer (e.g., internal versus external, government versus commercial). Application areas often overlap.
Arrow	The graphical presentation of an activity.
Arrow Diagramming Method (ADM)	A network diagramming technique in which activities are represented by arrows. The tails of the arrow represents the start, and the head represents the finish of the activity. Activities are connected at points called nodes to illustrate the sequence in which the activities are expected to be performed.

Assumptions	Assumptions are factors that, for planning purposes, are considered to be true, real, or certain. Assumptions affect all aspects of project planning, and are part of the progressive elaboration of the project. Project teams frequently identify, document, and validate assumptions as part of their planning process. Assumptions generally involve a degree of risk.
Backward Pass	The calculation of late finish dates and late start dates for the uncompleted portions of all network activities. Determined by working backwards through the network logic from the project's end date. The end date may be calculated in a forward pass or set by the customer or sponsor.
Bar Chart	A graphic display of schedule-related information. In the typical bar chart, activities or other project elements are listed down the left side of the chart, dates are shown across the top, and activity durations are shown as date-placed horizontal bars. They are also called Gantt charts.
Baseline	The original approved plan, plus or minus approved scope changes. Usually used with a modifier (e.g., cost baseline, schedule baseline, etc.)
Brainstorming	A general creativity technique that can be used to identify risks using a group of team members or subject-matter experts. Typically, a brainstorming session is structured so that each participant's ideas are recorded for later analysis. It is a tool of the risk identification process.
Budget at Completion (BAC)	The sum of the total budgets for a project.
Budgeted Cost of Work Performed (BCWP)	This term has been replaced with the term earned value.
Budgeted Cost of Work Schedule (BCWS)	This term has been replaced with the term planned value.
Calendar Unit	The smallest unit of time used in scheduling the project. Calendar units are generally in hours, days, or weeks, but can also be in shifts or even minutes. Used primarily in relationship to project management software.
Change Control Board (CCB)	A formally constituted group of stakeholders responsible for approving or rejecting changes to the project baselines.
Checklist	A listing of many possible risks that might occur on a project. It is used as a tool in the risk identification process. Checklists are comprehensive, listing several types of risk that have been encountered on prior projects.

Code of Accounts	Any numbering system used to uniquely identify each element of the work breakdown structure. See also chart of accounts.
Component	A constituent part, an element.
Constraint	Applicable restriction that will affect the performance of the project. Any factor that affects when an activity can be scheduled.
Contingency Planning	The development of a management plan that identifies alternative strategies to be used to ensure project success if specified risk events occur.
Contingency Reserve	The amount of money or time needed above the estimate to reduce the risk of overruns of project objectives to a level acceptable to the organization.
Contract	A contract is a mutually binding agreement that obligates the seller to provide the specified product and obligates the buyer to pay for it. Contracts generally fall into one of three broad categories: • Fixed-price or lump sum contracts—this category involves a fixed total price for a well-defined product. Fixed-price contracts may also include incentives for meeting or exceeding selected project objectives, such as schedule targets. • Cost-reimbursable contracts—this category of contract involves payment (reimbursement) to the contractor for its actual costs. Costs are usually classified as direct costs (costs incurred directly by the project, such as wages for members of the project team) and indirect costs (costs allocated to the project by the performing organization as a cost of doing business, such as salaries for corporate executives). Indirect costs are usually calculated as a percentage of direct costs. Cost-reimbursable contracts often include incentives for meeting or exceeding selected project objectives, such as schedule targets or total cost. • Time and material contracts—these contracts are a hybrid type of contractual arrangement that contain aspects of both cost-reimbursable and fixed-price-type arrangements. Time and material contracts resemble cost-type arrangements in that they are open ended, because the full value of the arrangement is not defined as the time of the award. Thus, time and material contracts can grow in contract value as if they were cost-reimbursable-type arrangements. Conversely, time and material arrangements can also resemble fixed-unit arrangements when, for example, the unit rates

	are preset by the buyer and seller, as when both parties agree on the rates for the category of "senior engineer".
Contract Administration	Managing the relationship with the seller.
Contract Closeout	Completion and settlement of the contract, including resolution of any open items.
Control	The process of comparing actual performance with planned performance, analyzing variances, evaluating possible alternatives, and taking appropriate corrective action as needed.
Control Account Plan (CAP)	Previously called a Cost Account Plan. The CAP is a management control point where the integration of scope and budget and schedule takes place, and where the measurement of performance will happen. CAPs are placed at selected management points of the work breakdown structure.
Control Charts	Control charts are a graphic display of the results, over time and against established control limits, of a process. They are used to determine if the process is "in control" or in need of adjustment.
Corrective Action	Changes made to bring expected future performance of the project in line with the plan.
Cost Budgeting	Allocating the cost estimates to individual work activities.
Cost Control	Controlling changes to the project budget.
Cost estimating	Developing an approximation (estimate) of the cost of the resources needed to complete project activities.
Cost of Quality	The costs incurred to ensure quality. The cost of quality includes quality planning, quality control, quality assurance, and rework.
Cost Performance Index (CPI)	The cost efficiency ratio of earned value to actual costs. CPI is often used to predict the magnitude of a possible cost overrun using the following formula: BAC/CPI = projected cost at completion. CPI = EV divided by AC.
Cost-Plus-Fixed Fee (CPFF) Contract	A type of contract where the buyer reimburses the seller for the seller's allowable costs (allowable costs are defined by the contract) plus a fixed amount of profit (fee).
Cost-Plus-Incentive-Fee (CPIF) Contract	A type of contract where the buyer reimburses the seller for the seller's allowable costs and the seller earns its profit if it meets defined performance criteria.
Cost Variance (CV)	1) Any difference between the budgeted cost of an activity and the actual cost of that activity. 2) In earned value, EV less ACWP = CV
Crashing	Taking action to decrease the total project duration

	after analyzing a number of alternatives to determine how to get the maximum duration compression for the least cost.
Critical Activity	Any activity on a critical path. Most commonly determined by using the critical path method. Although some activities are "crit dictionary sense, without being on the critical path, this meaning is seldom used in the project context.
Critical Path	The series of activities that determines the duration of the project. In a deterministic model, the critical path is usually defined as those activities with float less than or equal to a specified value, often zero. It is the longest path through the project. See critical path method.
Critical Path Method (CPM)	A network analysis technique used to predict project duration by analyzing which sequence of activities (which path) has the least amount of scheduling flexibility (the least amount of float). Early dates are calculated by means of a forward pass, using a specified start date. Late dates are calculated by means of a backward pass, starting from a specified completion date (usually the forward pass' calculated project early finish date).
Current Finish Date	The current estimate of the point in time when an activity will be completed.
Current Start Date	The current estimate of the point in time when an activity will begin.
Data Date (DD)	The date at which, or up to which, the project's reporting system has provided actual status and accomplishments. Also called as-of date.
Decision Tree Analysis	The decision tree is a diagram that describes a decision under consideration and the implications of choosing one or another of the available alternatives. It incorporates probabilities or risks and the costs or rewards of each logical path of events and future decisions.
Deliverable	Any measurable, tangible, verifiable outcome, result, or item that must be produced to complete a project or part of a project. Often sued more narrowly in reference to an external deliverable, which is a deliverable that is subject to approval by the project sponsor or customer.
Duration (DU)	The number of work periods required to complete an activity or other project element. Usually expressed as workdays or workweeks. Sometimes incorrectly equated with elapsed time.
Duration Compression	Shortening the project schedule without reducing the project scope. Duration compression is not always possible and often requires an increase in

	project cost.
Early Finish Date (EF)	In the critical path method, the earliest possible point in time on which the uncompleted portions of an activity (or the project) can finish, based on the network logic and any schedule constraints. Early finish dates can change as the project progresses and changes are made to the project plan.
Early Start Date (ES)	In the critical path method, the earliest possible point of time on which the uncompleted portions of an activity can start, based on the network logic and any schedule constraints. Early start dates can change as the project progresses and changes are made to the project plan.
Earned Value (EV)	The physical work accomplished plus the authorized budget for this work. The sum of the approved cost estimates for activities completed during a given period. Previously called the budgeted cost of work performed (BCWP) for an activity or group of activities.
Earned Value Management (EVM)	A method for integration scope, schedule, and resources, and for measuring project performance. It compares the amount pf work that was planned with what was actually earned with what was actually spent to determine if cost and schedule performance are as planned.
Element	One of the parts, substances, or principles that make up a compound or complex whole.
Estimate	An assessment of the likely quantitative result. Usually applied to project costs and durations and should always include some indication of accuracy (e.g., ± x percent). Usually used with a modifier (e.g., preliminary, conceptual, feasibility). Some application areas have specific modifiers that imply particular accuracy ranges.
Estimate at Completion (EAC)	The expected total cost of an activity, a group of activities, or the project when the defined scope of work has been completed. Most techniques for forecasting EAC include some adjustment of the original cost estimate, based on actual project performance to date.
Estimate to Complete (ETC)	The expected additional cost needed to complete an activity, a group of activities, or the project. Most techniques for forecasting ETC include some adjustment to the original estimate, based on project performance to date. Also called "estimated to
Event-on-Node	A network diagramming technique in which events are represented by boxes (or nodes) connected by arrows to show the sequence in which the events are

	to occur. Used in the original program evaluation and review technique (PERT).
Exception Report	Document that includes only major variations from plan, rather than all variations.
Fast Tracking	Compressing the project schedule by overlapping activities that would normally be done in sequence, such as design and construction.
Finish Date	A point of time associated with an activity's completion. Usually qualified by one of the following: actual, planned, estimated, scheduled, early, late, baseline, target, or current.
Finish-to-Finish (FF)	See logical relationship.
Finish-to-Start (FS)	See logical relationship.
Firm Fixed-Price (FFP)	A type of contract where the buyer pays the seller a set amount (as defined by the contract), regardless of the seller's costs.
Fixed-Price-Incentive-Fee (FPIF) Contract	A type of contract where the buyer pays the seller a set amount (as defined by the contract), and the seller can earn an additional amount if it meets defined performance criteria.
Float	The amount of time that an activity may be delayed from its early start without delaying the project finish date. Float is a mathematical calculation, and can change as the project progresses and changes are made to the project plan. Also called slack, total float, and path float.
Forward Pass	The calculation of the early start and early finish dates for the uncompleted portions of all network activities. See also network analysis and backward pass.
Free Float (FF)	The amount of time that an activity can be delayed without delaying the early start of any immediately following activities.
Functional Manager	A manager responsible for activities in a specialized department or function (e.g., marketing, manufacturing, engineering).
Functional Organization	An organization structure in which staff are grouped hierarchically by specialty (e.g., production, marketing, engineering, and accounting at the top level; with engineering, further divided into mechanical, civil, electrical, and others).
Gantt Chart	See bar chart.
Grade	A category or rank used to distinguish items that have the same functional use (e.g., hammer), but do not share the same requirements for quality (e.g., different hammers may need to withstand different amounts of force).
Graphical Evaluation and	A network analysis technique that allows for

Review Technique (GERT)	conditional and probabilistic treatment of logical relationships (i.e., some activities may not be performed).
Hammock	An aggregate or summary activity (a group of related activities is shown as one and reported at a summary level). A hammock may or may not have an internal sequence.
Hanger	An unintended break in a network path. Hangers are usually caused by missing activities or missing logical relationships.
Information Distribution	Making needed information available to project stakeholders in a timely manner.
Initiation	Authorizing the project or phase.
Integrated Change Control	Coordinating changes across the entire project.
Invitation for Bid (IFB)	Generally, this term is equivalent to request for proposal (RFP). However, in some application areas, it may have a narrower or more specific meaning.
Lag	A modification of a logical relationship that directs a delay in the successor task. For example, in a finish-to-start dependency with a ten-day lag, the successor activity cannot start until ten days after the predecessor has finished.
Late Finish Date (LF)	In the critical path method, the latest possible point in time that an activity may be completed without delaying a specified milestone (usually the project finish date).
Late Start Date (LS)	In the critical path method, the latest possible point in time that an activity may begin without delaying a specified milestone (usually the project finish date).
Lead	A modification of a logical relationship that allows an acceleration of the successor task. For example, in a finish-to-start dependency with a ten-day lead, the successor activity can start ten days before the predecessor has finished.
Lessons Learned	The learning gained from the process of performing the project. Lessons learned may be identified at any point. Also considered a project record.
Level of Effort (EOF)	Support-type activity (e.g., vendor or customer liaison) that does not readily lend itself to measurement of discrete accomplishments. It is generally characterized by a uniform rate of activity over a period of time determined by the activities it supports.
Life-Cycle Costing	The concept of including acquisition, operating, and disposal costs when evaluating various alternatives.
Line Manager	1) The manager of any group that actually makes a

	product or performs a service. 2) A functional manager.
Logic Diagram	See project network diagram.
Logical Relationship	A dependency between two project activities, or between a project activity and a milestone. See also precedence relationship. The four possible types of logical relationships are: • Finish-to-start—the initiation of work of the successor depends upon the completion of work of the predecessor. • Finish-to-finish—the completion of the work of the successor cannot finish until the completion of work of the predecessor. • Start-to-start—the initiation of work of the successor depends upon the initiation of the work of the predecessor. • Start-to-finish—the completion of the successor is dependent upon the initiation of the predecessor.
Loop	A network path that passes the same node twice. Loops cannot be analyzed using traditional network analysis techniques such as critical path method (CPM) and program evaluation and review technique (PERT). Loops are allowed in graphical evaluation and review technique (GERT).
Master Schedule	A summary-level schedule that identifies the major activities and key milestones. See also milestone schedule.
Matrix Organization	Any organizational structure in which the project manager shares responsibility with the functional managers for assigning priorities and for directing the work of individuals assigned to the project.
Milestone	A significant event in the project, usually completion of a major deliverable.
Milestone Schedule	A summary-level schedule that identifies the major milestone.
Monitoring	The capture, analysis, and reporting of project performance, usually as compared to plan.
Monte Carlo Analysis	A technique that performs a project simulation many times to calculate a distribution of likely results.
Near-Critical Activity	An activity that has low total float.
Network Analysis	The process of identifying early and late start and finish dates for the uncompleted portions of project activities. See also CPM, PERT, and GERT.
Network Logic	The collection of activity dependencies that makes up a project network diagram.
Network Path	Any continuous series of connected activities in a project network diagram.

Node	One of the defining points of a network; a junction point joined to some or all of the other dependency lines. See also arrow diagramming method and precedence diagramming method.
Organizational Breakdown Structure (OBS)	A description of the project organization arranged so as to relate work packages to organizational units.
Organizational Planning	Identifying, documenting, and assigning project roles, responsibilities, and reporting relationships.
Parametric Estimating	An estimating technique that uses a statistical relationship between historical data and other variables (e.g., square footage in construction, lines of code in software development) to calculate an estimate.
Pareto Diagram	A histogram, ordered by frequency of occurrence, that shows how many results were generated by each identified cause.
Path	A set of sequencing connected activities in a project network diagram.
Path Convergence	The node in the schedule where parallel paths merge or join. At that node, delays or elongation or any converging path can delay the project. In quantitative risk analysis of a schedule, significant risk may occur at this point.
Percent Complete (PC)	An estimate, expressed as a percent, of the amount of work that has been completed on an activity or a group of activities.
Performance Measurement Baseline	An approved plan against which deviations are compared for management control.
Performance Reporting	Collecting and disseminating performance information. This includes status reposting, progress measurement, and forecasting.
Performing Organization	The enterprise whose employees are most directly involved in doing the work of the project.
PERT Chart	The term is commonly used to refer to a project network diagram. See PERT for the traditional definition of PERT.
Planned Value (PV)	The physical work scheduled, plus the authorized budget to accomplish the scheduled work. Previously, this was called the budgeted costs for work scheduled (BCWS).
Precedence Diagram Method (PDM)	A network diagramming technique in which activities are represented by boxes (or nodes). Activities are linked by precedence relationships to show the sequence in which the activities are to be performed.
Precedence Relationship	The term used in the precedence diagramming method for a logical relationship. In current usage,

	however, precedence relationship, logical relationship, and dependency are widely used interchangeably, regardless of the diagramming method in use.
Predecessor Activity	1) In the arrow diagramming method, the activity that enters a node. 2) In the precedence diagramming method, the "from" activity.
Probability and Impact Matrix	A common way to determine whether a risk is considered low, moderate, or high by combining the two dimensions of a risk, its probability of occurrence, and its impact on objectives if it occurs.
Procurement Planning	Determining what to procure and when.
Product Scope	The features and functions that characterize a product or service.
Program	A group of related projects managed in a coordinated way. Programs usually include an element of ongoing work.
Program Evaluation and Review Technique (PERT)	An event-oriented network analysis technique used to estimate program duration when there is uncertainty in the individual activity duration estimates. PERT applies the critical path method using durations that are computed by a weighted average of optimistic, pessimistic, and most likely duration estimates. PERT computes the standard deviation of the completion date from those of the path's activity durations. Also known as the Method of Moments Analysis.
Project	A temporary endeavor undertaken to create product, service, or result.
Project Charter	A document issued by senior management that formally authorizes the existence of a project. And it provides the project manager with the authority to apply organizational resources to project activities.
Project Communications Management	A subset of project management that includes the processes required to ensure timely and appropriate generation, collection and dissemination, storage and ultimate disposition of project information. It consists of communications planning, information distribution, performance reporting, and administrative closure.
Project Cost Management	A subset of project management that includes the processes required to ensure that the project is completed within the approved budget. It consists of resource planning, cost estimating, cost budgeting, and cost control.
Project Human Resources management	A subset of project management that includes the processes required to make the most effective use of people involved with the project. It consists of organizational planning, staff acquisition, and team development.

Project Integration Management	A subset of project management that includes the processes required to ensure that the various elements of the project are properly coordinated. It consists of project plan development, project plan execution, and integrated change control.
Project Life Cycle	A collection of generally sequential project phases whose name and number are determined by the control needs of the organization or organizations involved in the project.
Project Management (PM)	The application of knowledge, skills, tools, and techniques to project activities to meet the project requirements.
Project Management Body of Knowledge (PMBOK)	An inclusive term that describes the sum of knowledge within the profession of project management. As with other professions—such as law, medicine, and accounting—the body of knowledge rests with the practitioners and academics that apply and advance it. The PMBOK includes proves, traditional practices that are widely applied, as well as innovative and advanced ones that have seen more limited use.
Project Management Professional	An individual certified as such by the Project Management Institute (PMI).
Project Management Software	A class of computer applications specifically designed to aid with planning and controlling project costs and schedules.
Project Management Team	The members of the project team who are directly involved in project management activities. On some smaller projects, the project management team may include virtually all of the project team members.
Project Manager (PM)	The individual responsible for managing a project.
Project Network Diagram	Any schematic display of the logical relationships of project activities. Always drawn from left to right to reflect project chronology. Often referred to as a PERT chart.
Project Phase	A collection of logically related project activities, usually culminating in the completion of a major deliverable.
Project Plan	A formal, approved document used to guide both project execution and project control. The primary uses of the project plan are to document planning assumptions and decisions, facilitate communication among stakeholders, and document approved scope, cost, and schedule baselines. A project plan may be summary or detailed.
Project Plan Development	Integrating and coordinating all project plans to create a consistent, coherent document.
Project Plan Execution	Carrying out the project plan by performing the activities include therein.

Project Planning	The development and maintenance of the project plan.
Project Procurement Management	A subset of project management that includes the processes required to acquire goods and services to attain project scope from outside the performing organization. It consists of procurement planning, solicitation planning, solicitation, source selection, contract administration, and contract closeout.
Project Quality Management	A subset of project management that includes the processes required to ensure that the project will satisfy the needs for which it was undertaken. It consists of quality planning, quality assurance, and quality control.
Project Risk Management	Risk management is the systematic process of identifying, analyzing, and responding to project risk. It includes maximizing the probability and consequences of positive events and minimizing the probability and consequences of events adverse to project objectives. It includes processes of risk management planning, risk identification, qualitative risk analysis, quantitative risk analysis, risk response planning, and risk monitoring and control.
Project Schedule	The planned dates for performing activities and the planned dates for meeting milestones.
Project Scope	The work that must be done to deliver a product with the specified features and functions.
Project Scope Management	A subset of project management that includes the processes required to ensure that the project includes all the work required, and only the work required, to complete the project successfully. It consists of initiation, scope planning, scope definition, scope verification, and scope change control.
Project Team Members	The people who report either directly or indirectly to the project manager.
Project Time Management	A subset of project management that includes the processes required to ensure timely completion of the project. It consists of activity definition, activity sequencing, activity duration estimating, schedule development, and schedule control.
Projectized Organization	Any organizational structure in which the project manager has full authority to assign priorities to direct the work of individuals assigned to the project.
Qualitative Risk Analysis	Performing a qualitative analysis of risks and conditions to prioritize their efforts on project objectives. It involves assessing the probability and impact of project risk (s) and using methods such as

	probability and impact matrix to classify risks into categories of high, moderate, and low for prioritized risk response planning.
Quantitative Risk Analysis	Measuring the probability and consequences of risks and estimating their implications for project objectives. Risks are characterized by probability distributions of possible outcomes. The process uses quantitative techniques such as simulation and decision tree analysis.
Quality Assurance (QA)	1) The process of evaluating overall project performance on a regular basis to provide confidence that the project will satisfy the relevant quality standards. 2) The organizational unit that is assigned responsibility for quality assurance.
Quality Control (QC)	1) The process of monitoring specific project results to determine if they comply with relevant quality standards and identifying ways to eliminate causes of unsatisfactory performance. 2) The organizational unit that is assigned responsibility for quality control.
Quality Planning	Identifying which quality standards are relevant to the project, and determining how to satisfy them.
Remaining Duration (RDU)	The time needed to complete an activity.
Request for Proposal (RFP)	A type of bid document used to solicit proposals from prospective sellers of products or services. In some application areas, it may have a narrower or ore specific meaning.
Request for Quotation (RFQ)	Generally, this term is equivalent to request for proposal. However, in some application areas, it may have a narrower or more specific meaning.
Reserve	A provision in the project plan to mitigate cost and/or schedule risk. Often used with a modifier (e.g., management reserve, contingency reserve) to provide further detail on what types of risk are meant to be mitigated. The specific meaning of the modified term varies by application area.
Residual Risk	A risk that remains after risk responses have been implemented.
Resource Planning	Determining what resources (people, materials, equipment) are needed in what quantities to perform project activities.
Responsibility Assignment Matrix (RAM)	A structure that relates the project organization structure to the work breakdown structure to help ensure that each element of the project's scope of work is assigned to a responsible individual.
Retainage	A portion of a contract payment that is held until contract completion to ensure full performance of the contract terms.

Rework	Action taken to bring a defective or nonconforming item into compliance with requirements or specifications.
Risk	An uncertain event or condition, if it occurs, has a positive or negative effect on a project's objectives.
Risk Acceptance	This technique of the risk response planning process indicates that the project team has decided not to change the project plan to deal with a risk, or is unable to identify any other suitable response strategy.
Risk Avoidance	Risk avoidance is changing the project plan to eliminate the risk or to protect the project objectives from its impact. It is a tool of the risk response planning process.
Risk Category	A source of potential risk reflecting technical, project management, organizational, or external sources.
Risk Database	A repository that provides for collection, maintenance, and analysis of data gathered and used in the risk management processes. A lessons-learned program uses a risk database. This is an output of the risk monitoring and control process.
Risk Event	A discrete occurrence that may affect the project to better or worse.
Risk Identification	Determining which risks might affect the project and documenting their characteristics. Tools used include brainstorming and checklists.
Risk Management Plan	Documents how the risk processes will be carried out during the project. This is the output of risk management planning.
Risk Management Planning	Deciding how to approach and plan risk management activities for a project.
Risk Mitigation	Risk mitigation seeks to reduce the probability and/or impact of a risk to below an acceptable threshold.
Risk Monitoring and Control	Monitoring residual risks, identifying new risks, executing risk reduction plans, and evaluating their effectiveness throughout the project life cycle.
Risk Response Plan	A document detailing all identified risks, including description, cause, probability of occurring, impacts on objectives, proposed responses, owners, and current status. Also known as risk register.
Risk Response Planning	Developing procedures and techniques to enhance opportunities and reduce threats to the project's objectives. The tools include avoidance, mitigation, transference, and acceptance.
Risk Transference	Risk transference is seeking to shift the impact of a risk to a third party together with ownership of the

	response.
S-Curve	Graphic display of cumulative costs, labor hours, percentage of work, or other quantities, plotted against time. The name derives from the S-like shape of the curve produced on a project that starts slowly, accelerates, and then tails off. Also a term for the cumulative likelihood distribution that is a result of s simulation, a tool of quantitative risk analysis.
Schedule Development	Analyzing activity sequences, activity durations, and resource requirements to create the project schedule.
Schedule Performance Index (SPI)	The schedule efficiency ratio of earned value accomplished against the planned value. The SPI describes what portion of the planned schedule was actually accomplished. The SPI = EV divided by PV.
Schedule Variance (SV)	1) Any difference between the scheduled completion of an activity and the actual completion of that activity. 2) In earned value, EV less BCWS = SV.
Scheduled Finish Date (SF)	The point in time that work was scheduled to finish on an activity. The scheduled finish date is normally within the range of dates delimited by the early finish date and the late finish date. It may reflect leveling or scarce resources.
Scheduled Start Date (SS)	The point in time that work was scheduled to start on an activity. The scheduled start date is normally within the range of dates delimited by the early start date and the late start date. It may reflect leveling of scarce resources.
Scope	The sum of the products and services to be provided as a project. See project scope and product scope.
Scope Change	Any change to the project scope. A scope change almost always requires an adjustment to the project cost and/or schedule.
Scope Change Control	Controlling changes to project scope.
Scope Definition	Subdividing the major deliverables into smaller, more manageable components to provide better control.
Scope Planning	The process of progressively elaborating the work of the project, which includes developing a written scope statement that includes the project justification, the major deliverables, and the project objectives.
Scope Statement	The scope statement provides a documented basis for making future project decisions and for confirming or developing common understanding of project scope among the stakeholders. As the project progresses, the scope statement may need to be revised or refined to reflect approved changes to the scope of the project.
Scope Verification	Formalizing acceptance of the project scope.

Secondary Risk	A risk that arises as a direct result of implementing a risk response.
Seller	The provider of goods or services to an organization.
Should-Cost Estimate	An estimate of the cost of a product or service used to provide an assessment of the reasonableness of a prospective contractor's proposed cost.
Simulation	A simulation uses a project model that translates the uncertainties specified at a detailed level into their potential impact on objectives that are expressed at the level of the total project. Project simulations use computer models and estimates of risk at a detailed level, and are typically performed using the Monte Carlo technique.
Slack	Term used in arrow diagramming method for float.
Solicitation	Obtaining quotations, bids, offers, or proposals as appropriate.
Solicitation Planning	Documenting product requirements and identifying potential source.
Source Selection	Choosing from among potential sellers.
Staff Acquisition	Getting needed human resources assigned to and working on the project.
Stakeholder	Individuals and organizations that are actively involved in the project, or whose interests may be positively or negatively affected as a result of project execution or project completion. They may also exert influence over the project and its results.
Start Date	A point in time associated with an activity's start, usually qualified by one of the following: actual, planned, estimated, scheduled, early, late, target, baseline, or current.
Statement of Work (SOW)	A narrative description of products or services to be supplied under contract.
Subnet	A subdivision of a project network diagram, usually representing some form of subproject.
Subproject	A smaller portion of the overall project.
Successor Activity	1) In the arrow diagramming method, the activity that departs a node. 2) In the precedence diagramming method, the "to" activity.
Target Completion Date (TC)	An imposed date that constraints or otherwise modified the network analysis.
Target Finish Date (TF)	The date that work is planned to finish on an activity.
Target Start Date (TS)	The date that work is planned to start on an activity.
Task	A generic term for work that is not included in the work breakdown structure, but potentially could be a further decomposition of work by the individuals responsible for that work. Also, lowest level of effort on a project.
Team Development	Developing individual and group competencies to

	enhance project performance.
Technical Performance Measurement	Technical performance measurement compares technical accomplishments during project execution to the project plan's schedule of technical achievement.
Time-Scaled Network Diagram	Any project network diagram drawn in such a way that the positioning and length of the activity represent its duration. Essentially, it is a bar chart that includes network logic.
Total Float (TF)	See float.
Total Quality Management (TQM)	A common approach to implementing a quality improvement program within an organization.
Triggers	Triggers, sometimes called risk symptoms or warning signs, are indications that a risk has occurred or is about to occur. Triggers may be discovered in the risk identification process and watched in the risk monitoring and control process.
Value Engineering (VE)	Value engineering is a creative approach used to optimize life-cycle costs, save time, increase profits, improve quality, expand market share, solve problems, and/or use resources more effectively.
Workaround	A response to a negative risk event. Distinguished from contingency plan in that a workaround is not planned in advance of the occurrence of the risk event.
Work Breakdown Structure (WBS)	A deliverable-oriented grouping of project elements that organizes and defines that total work scope of the project. Each descending level represents an increasingly detailed definition of the project work.
Work Item	Term no longer in common usage. Synonymous with activity.
Work Package	A deliverable at the lowest level of the work breakdown structure, when that deliverable may be assigned to another project manager to plan and execute. This may be accomplished through the use of a subproject where the work package may be further decomposed into activities.

REFERENCES

- Patrice Murphy. 1989, Pharmaceutical Project Management: Is It Different?
- John Kotter. 1990, A Force for Change: How leadership Differs from Management.
- Jeffrey Pfeffer. 1992, Managing with Power: Politics and Influence in Organizations.
- Robert Eccles et al. 1992, Beyond the Hype.
- International Organization for Standardization. 1994.
- American Heritage Dictionary of the English Language.
- Rodney Turner. 1992, The Handbook of Project-Based Management.
- The Guide to the Project Management Body of Knowledge. 2000.
- Howard Timms. 1966, The Production Function in Business.
- Terry Williams. 1996, Proceedings of the NATO Advanced Research Workshop on Managing and Modeling Complex Projects.
- Morris Hamburg. 1983, Statistical Analysis for Decision Making.
- Masaaki Imai. 1986, Kaizen: The Key to Japan's Competitive Success.
- James Lewis. 1991, Project Planning, Scheduling and Control.
- Paul Newbold. 1986, Principles of Management Science.

0-595-22073-8

www.ingramcontent.com/pod-product-compliance
Lightning Source LLC
Chambersburg PA
CBHW020738180526
45163CB00001B/278